COACHING
POSITIONAL PLAY

"Expansive Football" Attacking Tactics & Practices

Written by

PASQUALE CASÀ BASILE

Published by

COACHING POSITIONAL PLAY
"Expansive Football" Attacking Tactics & Practices

First Published October 2015 by SoccerTutor.com

Info@soccertutor.com | www.SoccerTutor.com
UK: 0208 1234 007 | **US:** (305) 767 4443 | **ROTW:** +44 208 1234 007

ISBN 978-1-910491-06-5

Original Spanish Publishers
Abfutbol ©, All Rights Reserved.

Spanish to English Translation
Abby Parkhouse - abbyparkhouse@yahoo.co.uk

Edited by
Alex Fitzgerald - SoccerTutor.com

Cover Design by
Alex Macrides, Think Out Of The Box Ltd.
Email: design@thinkootb.com Tel: +44 (0) 208 144 3550

Diagrams
Diagram designs by SoccerTutor.com. All the diagrams in this book have been created using SoccerTutor.com Tactics Manager Software available from
www.SoccerTutor.com

Note: While every effort has been made to ensure the technical accuracy of the content of this book, neither the author nor publishers can accept any responsibility for any injury or loss sustained as a result of the use of this material.

CONTENTS

DIAGRAM KEY

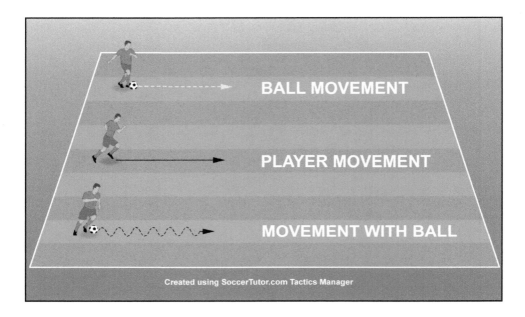

BALL MOVEMENT

PLAYER MOVEMENT

MOVEMENT WITH BALL

Created using SoccerTutor.com Tactics Manager

TACTICS FORMAT

Each tactical situation includes clear diagrams with supporting notes such as:

- Name of Tactical Situation
- Description of Tactical Situation
- Tactical Instructions (if applicable)

PRACTICE FORMAT

Each practice includes clear diagrams with supporting training notes such as:

- Name of Practice
- Objective of Practice
- Description of Practice
- Variation or Progression (if applicable)
- Coaching Points

OUR GAME MODEL FORMATION (4-3-3)

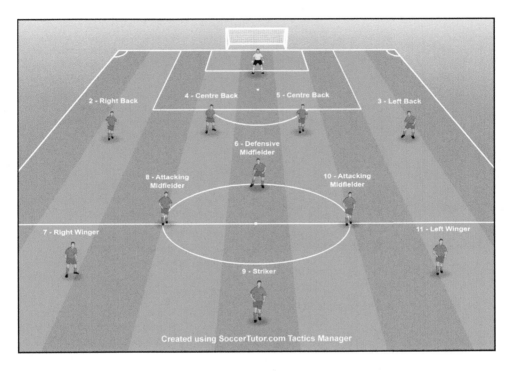

For our game model we use the 4-3-3 formation with 2 centre backs, 2 full backs, 1 defensive midfielder, 2 attacking midfielders, 2 wingers and 1 striker.

This 4-3-3 formation will be used throughout the book in the tactical analysis and training drills/practices. However, you can easily adapt all of the information and training to suit the formation that you use with your team.

There is no right formation and what is more important is the key concepts of our game model which we will explain in detail so you can help your team to play "Expansive Football".

COACH PROFILE

PASQUALE CASÀ BASILE
UEFA Pro Licence

- Catalan Football Federation Professeur for Level 1 Coaching Courses

- Head of Youth Development for FC Legirus Inter (Finland)

- Catalan Football Federation Professeur of Coaching Courses in Tactics, 2009-2011

- Coach at the Technical Centre of RCD Espanyol de Barcelona, 2005-2009

- Head Coach U19 Reus Deportiu (Catalonia), 2006-2009 (2006-2007 League Champions and promotion to highest level)

- Head Coach U15 Reus Deportiu, 2005-2006

- Head Coach U17 Gimnàstic de Tarragona (Spanish Segunda División), 2004-2005

- Head Coach Saavedra CEIP School of Fútbol Tarragona, 2004-2006

I have a UEFA Pro coaching, as well as being a specialist in tactics and team management. In the past I have trained a lot of clubs, in particular for four years at the technical centre for RCD Espanyol de Barcelona. I also worked in a technical project with the FC Barcelona Foundation. I am currently working as the Head of Youth Development for FC Legirus Inter in Finland.

This book was first published for the Italian market. I have also held many conferences on football and wrote several articles in trade magazines.

My work is usually to coordinate, facilitate and develop the work of the coaches and trainers of the youth teams, directing the development of tactics and periodization of the Spanish football model.

Going into more detail, the centre of all the work will be on the kids; they will train not only football, but also, through this method of teaching, we will help them to grow in personality, transmitting values and providing emotional education which is very important. To this we add the construction of socio-affective relations, fundamental to be not only good players, but also to be great people.

CHAPTER 1

The Idea:
Positional Attacking

POSITIONAL ATTACKING

"Positional attacking within our game model".

We will begin our journey along this theme by confirming that football is a marvellous game that each and every one of us has inside. A game in which nowhere is it written that the team that wins will always be the best, the biggest or the strongest, but instead the team that has moved closer to the prize that they aspire to, that wants it more, whose players have given their all with a coach who knows how to get everything from his players.

This sport, in its complexity, is full of microsystems that form and give life, feeding off each other. It is therefore endless and, we repeat, complex. The player, as Manuel Conde eloquently states, does not exist, he is contextual. He depends on many factors and is influenced by many variables.

On this basis, I'll bring up an article I read, *"Barca's game; Evolution or Revolution"*, in which the ex-footballer Michael Robinson and journalist John Carlin gave their personal vision of a possibly unrepeatable machine, the magnificent generation of footballers that are Barcelona, along with Guardiola, their orchestral maestro who knew exactly how to use Barca's football geniuses in perfect symphony and harmony.

This was the key that opened my Pandora's Box. It is curious how we spend our footballing lives talking about a moment of change after which all that went previously no longer matters, is thrown out and declared obsolete.

In these last few years the possession (and positional) football played by Barcelona has conquered the world and they have won everything.

Human beings, by their very nature and for their own wellbeing want to belong socially to a group, to something greater, to be part of or aspire to be a part of something bigger. Linking that to football, people follow Barcelona today in the same way as they followed Real Madrid during their hey day and Sacchi's Milan. In the present day, many teams try to imitate Barcelona's possession and positional play by playing with a 4-3-3 formation and by trying to play possession (although sometimes not positional) football.

It does not always work. The players cannot hold their shape and make progress towards the opposition's goal. There is something missing, something that does not work and in the long run they have negative results and lose matches. The team get stuck in a rut and the players lose confidence and trust in this style of play. You come to the conclusion that it is not enough just to want to play a passing game and realise that it must be trained, but that the players need to learn what to do, who to pass to and how to do it. Drills (or as Lillo says, "Situations") must be created and incorporated into training that reflect this passing game. The coach must also work on the resilience of the players so that they do not fall prey to frustration. How often do you see a team try to play a passing game and yet the midfielder lofts the ball forwards when they are closed down? The mental aspect should be incorporated into training sessions.

Even that is not enough; you must still have players who are ready for this type of game, although we strongly believe that anything can be trained.

Barcelona's possession and positional attacking game is a beautiful thing but that does not mean that they disregard other systems, such as Helenio Herrera's "Chain" or the offside game that Milan played under Saachi. Both were also good methods and defensively were also beautiful to watch. Like Barcelona's game – it was art.

At the end of the 1980's, Saachi's Italy gave us the 4-4-2, used by Capello with his Milan team in the 1990's. Then came Lippi's Juventus side with their 4-3-1-2 and everybody started playing that way. Later, Zaccheroni's Milan brought us a 3-4-1-2 and everybody followed. These days we are all following Barcelona, we want to belong to this group and imitate it, like a winning recipe, except we do not have the ingredients or the cooking instructions. What is curious is that all of the teams that we have just mentioned all had superstars up front i.e.. Van Basten, Baggio, Del Piero, George Weah. They also had top class midfielders i.e. Zidane, Boban, Totti and top class defenders i.e. Baresi, Ferrara, Maldini and Bergomi and we have not even mentioned the extraordinary goalkeepers behind them all.

These days Barcelona have Messi, Iniesta, Pique and many more with a football culture that these players carry inside of them, instilled in them from a very young age. Above all, they have a coach with the right profile, continuing the work started decades ago by Cruyff and carried on today by Luis Enrique. No matter how good the recipes that you have, if you do not have rich, healthy, fresh ingredients then the food will not taste good, and it will taste even worse if the chef does not know how to follow the recipe and add his own, distinctive touch.

In this book we will examine the way we look at attacking football, at attacking positions and combinations that will bring you closer to Barcelona's playing style, but at the same time closer to Real Madrid, Manchester United, Bayern Munich, Juventus and more top teams. To be great you must be eclectic, getting the best out of everybody and most importantly, integrate it into your knowledge and your very way of being.

We present our attacking positions within our tactical model of the attacking game which explains how to follow what we have referred to, developing the most important principles, forming new principles and providing some explanatory drills. We have named our model,

"Expansive Football", and the title will be better understood as we explain the way that we have developed it.

CHAPTER 2

DEVELOPING AN EFFECTIVE ATTACKING TACTICAL GAME

DEVELOPING AN EFFECTIVE ATTACKING TACTICAL GAME

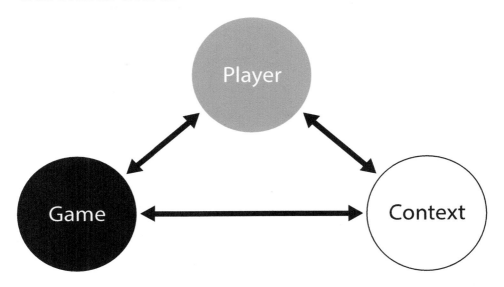

For a team to be great it is not enough to have excellent, prepared coaches whose knowledge expands beyond simply playing the game into psychology, coaching, group management etc. Nor is it enough to have a game model that is specific to the very last detail (we will explain what that is later). Above all a great team must have great players with the innate talent to make the difference.

There are footballers who, through complete dedication and hard work, substitute this innate talent for something different. We think that all footballers possess talent, not some more than others, but some different than others. What is very clear is that footballers make football, you cannot separate the game from the players. If we talk about the game we have to talk about the players, and the context through which they are governed. The player is the centre of everything, influencing the game and reciprocally, the context. At the same time the game and the context are influencing the player. We see that in this simple but clear graphic above.

The player can transform the game and the context. In turn, these two factors influence the player, making him evolve. We contend that the player, as a naturally intelligent human being can adapt. The richer the context and the game, the more he can positively influence them and improve them, creating an atmosphere, a micro-system that is better than when he started. Because of this, the process never stops changing and is in constant evolution.

The loop of continuous interactions between the game, footballer and context is not artificial, but is a natural process so a good coach should work on strengthening this loop through his work. He should be the creator and the enhancer of this natural process.

NURTURING THE PLAYERS

The coach is like a horticulturist who nurtures his plants, cares for them and lets the inner nature of a plant express what it has inside. Outside influences such as the sun and rain will do the rest and help it to grow. As much as it hurts us, we are not the real protagonists of this great and marvellous thing that is football, the players are.

Our role is to guide them and help them express what they have inside. For example, a one year old child begins to walk after first learning to crawl. The parent must first help the child learn to stand in order that they may walk, but it is the child that carries the inner instinct to walk and has the capability to walk. It is the child's inner nature that allows them to achieve it. We, the parents, merely help them to achieve this goal. The coach should do the same with his players.

By this we mean that we, as coaches, cannot impose fixed and determined tactics, prefabricated so that all teams play the same way because football is about interaction between the game, the players and the context. This is always different because there are always distinct realities that change from moment to moment. We must begin with the players, as Oscar Cano says, starting by observing how they function individually in order to discover the possibilities for interaction between them. You must let them be a player. This does not mean that you should let them do whatever they want by letting them play with total freedom, but by finding out what it is that they want to do, seeing how they use and express their best resources, which links strongly to their best capabilities. After that, you can demand them to be all that they can be and what they can become. The coach should then look for the most appropriate tactical strategy for them that is well adjusted to their characteristics and has the objective of exploiting their potential. You must respect the individual natures of the players while at the same time utilising their capabilities and qualities.

Consequently, we as coaches should never stifle the creativity of a player. Football is so incredible because there are creative players, not robots, who do extraordinary things. When you least expect it, the player that you thought was not really in the game will suddenly pull a rabbit out of the hat. These are the footballers who make the difference; it is this minority that makes the difference. We doubt that anyone could take that from a player like Messi and make him an automaton or shackle him, nor to Iniesta, Xavi, Isco or Pirlo, nor do we need to do it because, as Oscar Cano states:

"There are players who improve the context for everybody with each ball that they touch".

ORGANISED CHAOS

We should have a series of movements outlined, code named "Mechanical-non-mechanical" (Xavier Tamarit) that the players learn through constant interactions and which, to begin with, will be highly disorganised. The coaches should organise these movements and the players should be aware of them and recognise them. As a result, Manual Conde says, a team with high synergy will grow, creating a global tactical code to establish their collective function without restraining any player. But as we know with chaos theory, we must coordinate to create an order within the chaos. Unpredictability and uncertainty rule in football.

Jesus Pino states, *"For the talent to explode they need a tactical context that favours them, that allows the players' games to emerge and be seen. It is important for the coaches to let the players be players, within this context. This tactical environment allows for both giving and receiving. One player improves another and vice versa.*

Do Barcelona play well because they play spectacular combination football? No, that

is the style. Barcelona play well because they comply with the fundamental principles of football and correctly execute the required and appropriate technical actions for each moment, situation and game phase, whether it be attack, defence or transitional and always with the objective of winning." Jesus Cuadrado Pino continues, *"When the situation requires them to form a wall, they form a wall that is technically correct. When a low cross comes in after a dummy from the opposition, a teammate is in the space created by the dummy having read what the opposition is doing and the central defenders are in the correct positions and are oriented correctly in order to deal with it."*

The style will be the type of tactics that a coach uses with his team. Some styles are more attractive than others. Let me ask you a question: When Di Matteo's Chelsea team beat Barcelona in the final of the Champions League in 2012 did they play well? It is true that their style was not as spectacular as that of Barcelona but did they not follow all of the fundamental principles and technical-tactical specifications relating to their style of play? True, they were too defensive in their game, packing zone one with very tight lines, doubling up on defensive marking, launching very few counter attacks, but they played their game well and it crowned them champions of Europe in spite of the lesser individual and collective quality of their team.

HOW WE CAN ACHIEVE IT

Within this book we demonstrate how you can play attacking, attractive, passing football that complies tactically and technically with the fundamental principals of football.

POSITIONAL ATTACK

This type of attack (positional) is found in the attacking phase, when we are in possession of the ball. It is an organised attack that involves combined passing movements using a large number of passes, changes of direction and the intervention of many players. Some players are in support and others are on the break, creating spaces to ensure that possession is kept and progression is made with the final objective of scoring a goal. It is a type of attack that needs structure and continuous geometrical formations; triangles, rhombus etc. This is why it is positional, because we need the combination of various players in specific tactical positions in order to accomplish it.

EXPANSIVE AND PROGRESSION OF TIME AND SPACE

We want a technical-tactical combination of the aspects of space and time aimed towards progressing in the game and achieving a better result as a consequence. A good positional attack consists of invading and conquering the space on the pitch by making the pitch bigger, keeping the outside players in wide, deep, diagonal positions with the inside players floating in staggered positions. This is the beginning.

By making the pitch bigger, by moving the ball with changes in position, direction and from one side to the other (switching play), passing wide and deep we progress towards the objective of scoring a goal. We occupy the opponent's half, expanding ourselves into their half of the pitch using width and diagonal balls in order to penetrate their "Castle".

EXPANSIVE FOOTBALL

1. Scoring goals is fundamental, therefore we must repeat that when we look for width, we must always look to make progress forwards (in depth).

2. The aim of keeping possession of the ball with the secondary objective of scoring a goal. For example when a game is out of control and we need to calm it down, or when we are winning by a certain margin, the opponents are down to ten men and are very tired and we want to expend less energy to aid recuperation we can play a good possession game, making the ball run, not the players. These are the reasons why we need to play a good possession game.

First of all, to begin playing "Expansive Football" with the primary objective of scoring a goal, we should choose a formation and playing positions. In this case we have chosen the 4-3-3 formation in attack as it is a formation that lends itself to this type of positional attack, playing inside, outside, and within triangles etc.

We initiate the play from the back, always remembering this important concept:

Association is a vehicle for the game.

UNDERSTANDING PLAYER ATTRIBUTES

It is important to understand that in order to play "Expansive Football" efficiently we must circulate the ball quickly which means that we must have a good positional game.

It is essential that a player knows where his teammates are going to be when he receives the ball so that he can provide continuity to the game. We know that there are two types of pass; to feet or into space. These phases depend not only on the quality of the passer (if he prefers to pass long or short) or the specific game situation (e.g. If there is a defender close by who may intercept the pass) but also on the player receiving the ball. For instance Iniesta usually receives the ball to his feet whereas Fernando Torres usually runs onto a ball played into space. There are also factors such as time, keeping possession, risk percentage etc. It is therefore essential that each player knows what 'types' of players his teammates are, how they behave and, most importantly, how to 'interact' with them (what passes they prefer to receive). It is important to know the solutions that each player is likely to provide to solve a situation.

We will control the game with this type of positional attack but we must not forget that the ultimate objective is to score a goal. This is why pressing forward wide and deep, looking for progression and finding and occupying space in this type of attack is vital. Time is also vital.

THE TIME ASPECT

Time is determined and influenced by the space and context within it. Progression within the space is as important as the time within it. A free zone will always temporarily give you more time to play so in "Expansive Football"

we look to attack the passive zones, moving the ball from one side to the other. We will find less space the closer we get to the opponent's goal and therefore have less time to think and execute our actions.

With "Expansive Football" we gain time by using the free spaces but there is no need to be hasty, there is still time to think. The time that we have is influenced by two factors:

1. Ourselves performing the actions quickly, our attacking quality and our use of the open spaces.

2. The speed with which our opponents can organise and regroup defensively to block the open spaces.

We should consider time as something to master, as important as any numerical superiority, positioning or quality that we may have. Mastering time can make the difference as much as anything else. We know that time is relative. Three seconds on the ball is different for Iniesta than say, Gravesen or two seconds with Xavi on the ball against two seconds for Ballesteros without, or two seconds for Sergio Ramos on the ball against two seconds to Gattuso without it. This time can tip the balance in our favour.

Time is not only about quantity but quality. It should go hand in hand with space, to a time and place where the two become one. We are saying that it is not enough to simply perform the quick technical actions within an opponent's free zone. We have to look for the ideal moment in which to unite these two variables.

As Robert Moreno exemplified, a pass made into space for a player who has not escaped his marker is wrong at a decisional level, even if the execution is quick, the player will not

reach the ball in time. Or if a player loses his marker close to the player with the ball it is wrong at a decisional level as the opponent can easily anticipate the pass and intercept the ball and be in position before the ball is played and be waiting for it. Another example of bad decision making is when after receiving the ball, we already have the defender on top of us and are unable to perform a technical-tactical action, thus unable to gain an advantage or progress.

Robert Moreno expresses it well:
"Determining the opportune moment to perform each action can only be achieved through training and coordination between the elements of the team. There is no such thing as an identical moment for 2 different players. There are solutions that are the same but will always be applied differently by each player".

The ball and the player receiving the ball should "travel" together and both find themselves in the same place.

You see that "Expansive Football" is a type of positional attack that takes the movement of the players into account more than the system. You can play 4-4-2, 4-2-3-1 or 4-3-3 but what actually matters is the movement of the players. With this type of attack our opponents can use any system or game model against us and as long as we circulate the ball from one side to the other, find space and gaps in the defence created by our movement, we can progress and penetrate.

Our method of play must be guided by concepts, not by set positions on the pitch nor formations, as you can develop the same concepts that fit any system. As we have said before, the objective is always to be able to control the game through the application of the principals of our game model. As a great Argentinian coach once said, *"Formations are just telephone numbers"*.

Controlling the game does not simply mean having more time on the ball to move it around the pitch, but making everything more difficult for the opponent. We want to be the protagonists and this means taking the initiative, controlling the game and imposing our football style on our opponents with the objective of winning.

Building Up Play from the Back

Passing Out from the Goalkeeper to the Full Back with Good Support Play

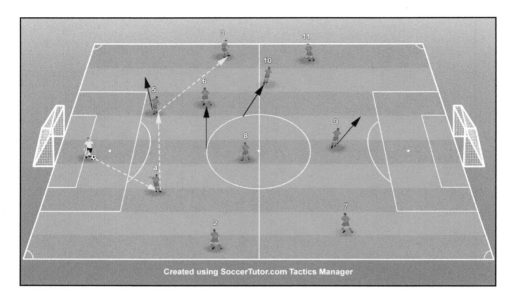

Created using SoccerTutor.com Tactics Manager

The combination starts with the goalkeeper passing to the centre back (4) who passes to the other centre back (5). The aim is to pass the ball to one of the wide men.

The fundamental principle of this tactic is that the ball is always played out wide with supporting players helping to move the ball forward, providing continuity and security. The players nearest the player with the ball should be continuously moving within passing range to the ball carrier.

Tactical Instructions
(The Full Back in Possession)

- The goalkeeper should stand outside of the 6 yard box and in line with the ball carrier to provide an emergency passing option.

- The centre back (5) stays in a deep position to provide support and security.

- The defensive midfielder (6) should be close to the ball to provide continuity.

- One attacking midfielder (8) stays central, supporting the wide players.

- The other attacking midfielder (10) moves diagonally to provide support forwards for the full back (3).

Building Up Play Using the Defensive Midfielder

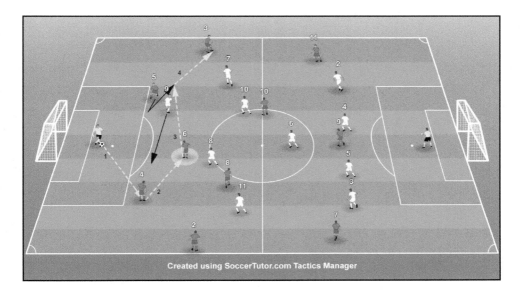

Created using SoccerTutor.com Tactics Manager

In this example, the initial ball is played out by the goalkeeper, and we notice that the red full backs (2 and 3) are playing very wide with the centre backs (4 and 5) also wide apart. The defensive midfielder (6) is slightly higher up the pitch and the goalkeeper is in the centre of the penalty area, creating a rhombus between these four players. They can combine easily; goalkeeper -> centre back -> centre back or goalkeeper -> centre back -> defensive midfielder -> centre back. This works if the opponents are not pressing and are waiting for us in the middle third.

If the opposing team are covering one of the flanks and have a player tactically marking our attacking midfielder on that side to force us to move the ball to the other wing where they have strong players who press and tackle well, we would start with the attacking midfielder who is not being closely marked. We would use the defensive midfielder to draw the marker away from the attacking midfielder and move the ball out wide in this way. At the

same time the midfielders should push up and the defensive midfielder move backwards to create doubt in the mind of the player marking our attacking midfielder. Additionally, the player marking our midfielder will be uncertain whether to move towards the player about to receive the ball. The defensive midfielder should be positioned in the passage that the ball is being played through to create a numerical superiority and facilitate these doubts in the opposition's mind.

We see in the diagram that the opposition's No.8 does not know whether to mark our defensive midfielder (6) or attacking midfielder (10) and is left in the middle of the two.

Building Up Play When the Defensive Midfielder is Marked Closely

If the opposition are closely marking the defensive midfielder (6) and are ready to anticipate and intercept the pass, we would position the attacking midfielder (8), winger (7) and the full back near the flank, creating a 3v1 situation.

The unmarked centre back (4) receives the pass from the goalkeeper and is unable to pass to the defensive midfielder as the white No.8 has stayed with him, so he dribbles towards the opponent (11) marking the closest winger, drawing him in. As the No.11 moves closer, the defender plays the ball to the attacking midfielder (8) who plays the ball straight to the advancing full back (2), as shown in the diagram. We have now successfully broken through the pressure and can attack in the opposition's half.

Building Up Play Against the Opposition's High Press (2 Markers)

Created using SoccerTutor.com Tactics Manager

If the opposition press high up the pitch and their forwards (9 and 10) mark our centre backs (4 and 5), the defensive midfielder (6) drops back, creating a flat back three.

Remember that we always stagger the midfielders diagonally in order to a create a numerical superiority, making sure that they do not take their markers too close to the player with the ball, diminishing his space and time. These angles are highlighted in the diagram with players No.6, No.8 and No.8 at diagonal angles to each other.

When the defensive midfielder (6) receives the ball, he passes to the closest midfielder (8) who then has two options:

1.   If there is no marker, he passes the ball straight to the full back. In some cases this might be after dribbling in his direction in order to draw his marker away and free him up).

2.   If he is closely marked, he passes to the centre back (5) and he can play it out wide.

Building Up Play Against the Opposition's High Press (3 Markers)

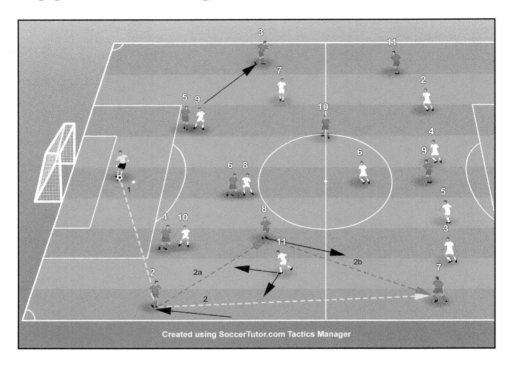

Created using SoccerTutor.com Tactics Manager

If the opposition use three players to press high up the pitch who are closely marking the centre backs (4 and 5) and the defensive midfielder (6), then one of the full backs should drop back to make it easier for the goalkeeper to pass to him. When the full back (2) receives the ball he has two options:

1. If an opponent (11) would intercept a pass down the line to the winger, he should pass to a midfielder (No.8 in diagram) who can lay the ball off to the winger (7).

2. If an opponent would intercept a pass to the midfielder (8), he should pass directly to the winger.

In both cases, after making the pass the midfielder (8) should stay close to the wide player to help move the ball across the pitch. The objective is always to get the ball out wide to the wingers. All of the players should be providing the appropriate support to the player with the ball according to the "Expansive Football" model, especially when the wide players are in possession of the ball.

It is important to make sure that we have a numerical superiority in and around the ball zone with the defensive midfielder dropping back and staggering the midfielders within an optimum distance of the player with the ball.

The players must be in the correct positions and oriented correctly so that they are always available in every situation in order to be effective and efficient during every move.

Using the Goalkeeper to Create a Numerical Superiority at the Back

Created using SoccerTutor.com Tactics Manager

The collaboration of the goalkeeper is very important as he can serve as an additional outfield player at any moment and always provides us with a numerical advantage at the back.

As shown in the diagram, when the goalkeeper passes to the available defender (4), the centre back is immediately closed down by an opponent so passes inside to the defensive midfielder (6). The defensive midfielder sees that there is an opponent behind him (10) so he passes back to the unmarked goalkeeper.

This example shown in the diagram illustrates why the goalkeeper is so important. The goalkeeper can control the ball and dribble towards the defender he wants to pass to, drawing the opponent (white 9) in who he takes the bait and moves to close down the goalkeeper. This leaves the centre back (5) free of marking and the goalkeeper quickly passes to him.

The centre back (5) then makes the same move by dribbling the ball towards the flank to draw an opponent (7) away from the full back so the team are finally able to play the ball out wide.

"Expansive Football Concepts"

Expansive Football - The Second Phase

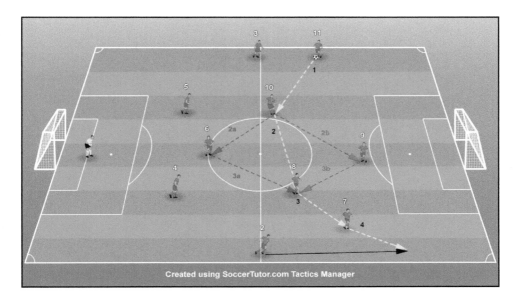

Created using SoccerTutor.com Tactics Manager

We now enter into the second phase of *"Expansive Football"*. As we said before, after looking at the width we must focus on depth. The full back must connect with the winger down his flank. Here there is another sequence of movements, always searching for support to give the game some continuity:

Tactical Instructions

- The full back (3) on the same flank moves further up and overlaps (if the winger is not already close to the byline).

- One attacking midfielder provides support from a deep defensive position. The other one provides support staying close by for continuity

- The defensive midfielder (6) provides support and security

- The striker moves vertically, providing deep attacking support.

If the winger (11) is unable to pass to the full back (3) on the overlap, he moves the ball back inside and away from where the opposition have concentrated their players, thus decongesting the zone. We must ensure that we keep possession of the ball even if that means going backwards and moving into the logical positions as directed by our initial organisational plan.

The winger passes inside to an attacking midfielder (10) who then passes to the other attacking midfielder (8), the defensive midfielder (6) or the striker (9) who lays it off to a midfielder. The attacking midfielder (8) passes the ball out wide enabling the winger to connect with the overlapping full back. Notice how all of the players supporting the player with the ball are staggered and covering in order to provide continuity, remembering to stay at the optimum distance so as not to draw their marker too close to the player with the ball and reduce his space.

Two Vital Expansive Football Concepts

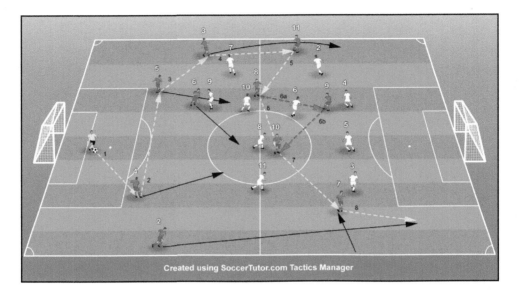

Created using SoccerTutor.com Tactics Manager

Notice that there is always width and depth in each situation, invading and conquering the opposition's half.

It is important to highlight two vital concepts of "Expansive Football" which are:

1. Play between the opponent's defensive and midfield lines (especially the central players).

2. Take advantage of the wide areas left open by the opposition, uniting against a compact defensive group by creating space through movement both in the centre of the pitch and on the flanks. This is why we should use the width of the pitch, moving the ball from one side to another if necessary until we can make progress up the pitch. We work as much in the initiation-creation zone as the creation-finalisation zone in order to continue moving the ball forwards and penetrate the opposition's defence, as shown in the diagram:

This is achieved through continuity of play, moving the ball quickly and ensuring that constant support is available to whoever has the ball.

There are 3 support players who are always close by in all directions for security and in case of emergency:

- The last defender (for security and in case of emergency).

- Close support behind the player with the ball (for continuity).

- Deep attacking support (vertically high up the pitch).

The Role of the Defensive Midfielder

The Pros and Cons of Playing With a Defensive Midfielder

Created using SoccerTutor.com Tactics Manager

It is important to highlight that in order to circulate the ball in a more efficient and effective way you can avoid using the defensive midfielder to advance, although he should be ready to be used if necessary.

The tactical context may permit the ball to be played directly to an attacking midfielder or a winger. It is more beneficial for the attacking midfielders to play the ball between themselves, or play winger -> attacking midfielder -> winger without using the defensive midfielder in order to get the ball out wide faster and give the opposition's defence less time to regroup. The defensive midfielder should always stay behind the ball to provide the support and security necessary to play "Expansive football" correctly.

There are pros and cons to playing with a defensive midfielder.

- **PROS:** As the defensive midfielder sits deeper and is more central, he has a broader view of the whole pitch so can see and pass to unmarked teammates more easily as he is unlikely to be as closely marked as the attacking midfielders. Secondly, when the opponent is pegged back in their own half and the defensive midfielder is close by, one of the attacking players can play a one-two with him and instantly make a move around their marker to gain some ground and find more space (ensuring that they stay onside).

- **CONS:** He can occasionally slow down the circulation of the ball by intervening and playing shorter passes. This is important if we are high up the pitch and we do not want to be playing the ball backwards, but are always looking to progress forwards.

The Defensive Midfielder Used as an 'Escape Valve'

Another good reason to play with a defensive midfielder is so when the ball is out on the flank and the attacking midfielder (No.10 in diagram) has moved closer to provide support or create a 3v1/2v1 situation, the defensive midfielder (6) can be available as an "escape valve" to decongest the game as it is likely that the other attacking midfielder will be tightly marked.

The defensive midfielder can use the space to spread the ball across to the other side of the pitch, playing "Expansive Football", as we see in this diagram.

The Defensive Midfielder Plays a Long Pass to the Flank

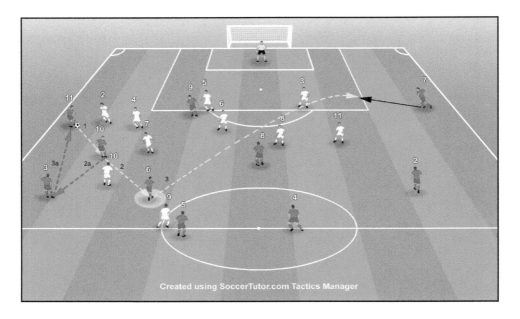

This is one of the few situations in which the defensive midfielder can play a long high ball to the opposite flank, bypassing the opposition's defenders who are all grouped in a specific zone.

After a quick sequence of passes to draw the defence into the zone, the defensive midfielder (6) can quickly spread the ball across the pitch to a teammate in space, as demonstrated in this diagram.

Support Play When the Ball is Out Wide

Support Play When the Ball is Out Wide - Roles and Responsibilities

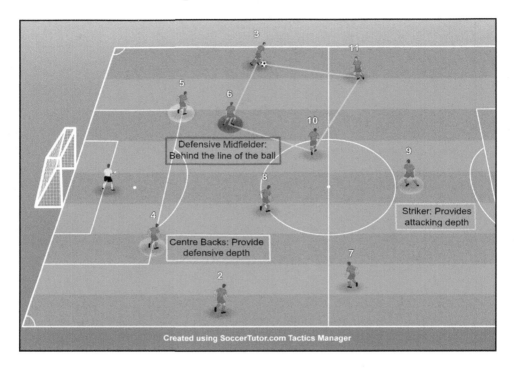

Created using SoccerTutor.com Tactics Manager

When the ball is out wide with the full back, the centre backs and the goalkeeper provide defensive depth and emergency support, but do push forwards into space as the attack progresses. The closer we get to the goal the less space we will have.

The defensive midfielder (6) should stay close by and behind the ball, as should the attacking midfielder on that side (10) when the winger has the ball out wide and the full back is moving up to overlap. The defensive midfielder is behind the line of the ball to provide continuity or, if we lose the ball, to apply pressure or provide cover.

Notice how the full back (3), winger (11), defensive midfielder (6) and the attacking midfielder (10) have created a rhombus, giving us a numerical superiority, with passes also available to the opposite full back or the striker.

The defensive midfielder (6) and attacking midfielder (10) should not be in line with the other players so as not to block their lines of sight, and therefore impede passes being played. We must remember that we also have the striker and goalkeeper providing depth (attacking and defending) respectively.

Support Play When the Ball is Out Wide - Roles and Responsibilities (2)

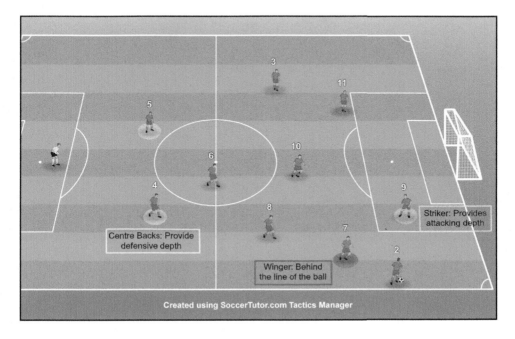

In this situation the winger (7) is providing support behind the ball when the full back overlaps him down the right flank. He has the same aim, which is to provide support and cover in case the ball is lost.

The striker (9), the goalkeeper and the attacking midfielder (8) are also in support, although this time, as they are closer to the opposition's goal, there is less distance between them.

Switching Play

KEY CONCEPTS WHEN SWITCHING PLAY IN EXPANSIVE FOOTBALL

SWITCHING PLAY

It is important to highlight that a key concept of "Expansive Football" is that if the ball comes from the wing, it should be played either forwards or over to the opposite side with a cross field pass.

By moving the ball from one side to the other you will create an imbalance in the opponent's defensive unit. Through moving the ball from one flank to the other and back to the middle you can begin to penetrate, using a series of movements to look for the attacking pass in behind the defensive line.

NO HORIZONTAL PASSES

Another important thing to note when playing "Expansive Football" is that no horizontal passes should be played during a wide attacking move as they are easy for the opponent to intercept. Our players should not be horizontal to each other and should be staggered and available for a diagonal pass along different lines so they are not closed down by an opponent. The players should be aware of their staggered positions (whether individually or zonally) for both attacking and defensive moves so that there are always passing options for the player with the ball, whilst making it more difficult for the opposition to man mark us.

There are distinct types of passes to use in this type of positional attack. Short passes should be used in tight spaces, whereas if we want to play the balls to zones that are further away, long flat passes should be used. The passes should also be technically correct, accurate and played with the necessary strength to facilitate a quick passing game. If a poor pass

is made it is harder for the receiver to get the ball under control and he can be closed down by an opponent. As Oscar Cano reflects, *"A pass is successful if it is received by the intended recipient, who must receive a gift of a pass not a problem of a pass".*

There should be continuous changes in direction using the "Expansive Football" model. With constant changes in direction you will avoid being trapped by the opposition who will be trying to create a numerical advantage in the zone where the ball is. Using these types of passes you can decongest these zones and look for space in passive zones further up field. We must pass the ball in a way that confuses the opposition so that we can change their organisation or try to concentrate them in one area so that we can move the ball quickly into another area where there is space to exploit.

We know that we must incorporate the full backs and centre backs to move higher up the pitch. Every player that we add to the attack forces one of the opposition's players to retreat to mark him, making us less vulnerable to being at a numerical disadvantage if the opposition counter attack.

Attacking With the Winger in an Advanced Position

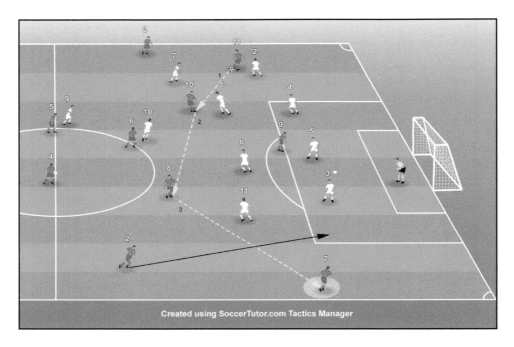

From this position the winger (11) can decide to do one of the following:

- Cross the ball into the penalty area if his teammates have made well timed runs.

- Pass backwards to a teammate in a supporting position (to No.10 as shown in the diagram).

- Perform a piece of individual skill to try and beat his direct opponent.

The wide player on the opposite flank (the right winger No.7) is in a supportive position near the sideline because it is possible that he will receive the ball and be able to do one of the following:

- Cross, shoot, or perform an individual or group skill (a one-two, triangles etc.).

- Play "Expansive Football", that is, by cutting inside or passing inside to try and penetrate in another area of the pitch.

- The midfielders can help the wide players advance by creating a 3v1 situation, using different combinations against the opposing defender: one-twos, triangles, overlapping etc.

When a winger moves inside in support looking for the ball, the full back can move up to occupy the space that has been created. Sometimes however, the winger will stay out on the wing because he has intelligently seen that his marker has moved towards the opposite side of the pitch where the ball is. So the full back on that side can break forwards, running inside the winger to make use of the space that has opened up, on the break. We see this in the diagram above.

Creating a Numerical Advantage on the Flank (Overlapping Full Back)

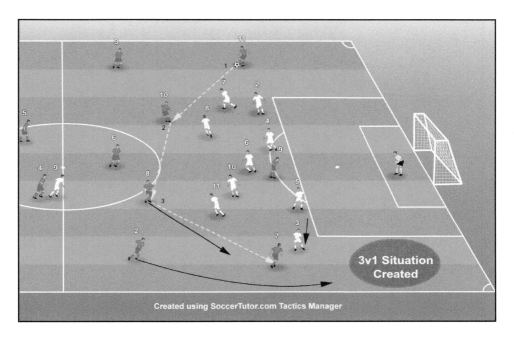

3v1 Situation Created

Created using SoccerTutor.com Tactics Manager

If there is an equality in numbers of players in and around the ball zone, we move the ball to the opposite side of the pitch (switch the play) by playing "Expansive Football" in order to search for a space where we do have a numerical advantage and can create a 2v1, 3v1 or 3v2 situation.

We need to find the easiest way to progress towards the opponent's goal, whether that be through the centre of the pitch or down the opposite flank.

We see in the diagram above how the winger (7) on the opposite flank, with support from inside and with the involvement of the full back (2), can help create a 3v1 situation with an overlapping run.

It is important that the full back pushes

forward when the ball is out wide, giving us a numerical advantage with the support of the attacking midfielder (8) and the winger (7).

Through this positioning we will have a 3v1 advantage against the opposition full back or 3v2 if he has cover.

If the full back is unable to push forward we should still have a 2v1 advantage with the winger and the midfielder (8).

Switching Play When the Opposition Condenses the Space on the Flank

3v3 on Flank = Switch Play

Created using SoccerTutor.com Tactics Manager

In the diagram above we analyse the opposition's defensive movement.

The opposing team have utilised their defensive tactic of covering and doubling up on marking, so therefore have a numerical equality near the flank (3v3 as shown in the diagram).

The opposition have condensed the area near the flank (the ball zone) and are making any progression nearly impossible for the attacking team.

The aim here is to switch the play out to the other flank and look for unmarked teammates in space who can progress further into the opponent's half and eventually in behind their defence.

In the diagram it shows the right winger (7) pass back to the attacking midfielder (8) who is in a supporting position. No.8 then passes across to the No.10 who is in a central position. From there, the No.10 is able to complete the switch of play by passing out wide to the left winger (11).

After the switch of play we now have a 2v1 numerical advantage on the flank for the attacking team to exploit. The left back (3) makes an overlapping run to receive in space.

Diagonal Break Away - 'The Taglio'

We use a very effective tactic called the 'taglio'. When the midfielder (8) receives the ball, he passes to the striker who plays it to the other midfielder and then moves into space, taking his marker with him, or at least away from the player with the ball.

The space created by this movement can be occupied by the midfielder who played the initial pass, performing a 'taglio' which is a diagonal break (run) made by the striker and the midfielder in opposite directions at the same time, as shown in the diagram by No.8 and No.9:

Diagonal Break Away - 'The Taglio' (Continued)

Created using SoccerTutor.com Tactics Manager

When the midfielder (10) receives the ball he has three passing options:

1. Pass diagonally to the striker who has lost his marker by moving up to support before breaking deeper to "go dark" *(see page 39 for full explanation)*. If the striker receives the ball he can shoot, or if he is closed down, he can play it to the other midfielder (8).

2. Pass forward to the breaking midfielder (8). If the No.8 is closed down by an opponent he can play a one-two with the striker (9) or pass to the winger penetrating the area (11).

3. Pass wide to the winger (11) who is being overlapped by the full back (3).

The decision making process depends solely on the individual situation e.g. If his teammates are marked, if they are well positioned, if they have the space to receive/play the ball etc. The midfielder must then decide who to pass to or which one of the three passing options to make. All three options are displayed in the diagram:

Playing a 'Wide Game' to Stretch the Opposition (1)

Space on the Flank

Created using SoccerTutor.com Tactics Manager

In addition to attacking width, we always want to have players high up the pitch and at a diagonal angle. This allows us to play forwards and to make it easy for a player to return the ball to either the player who passed it to him, a different player or, if he can, out wide. It is important to pass to a player facing you if you have your back to goal for two reasons:

1. It may not be easy to turn as there is probably an opponent directly behind you.

2. The recipient has a better view of the whole pitch and can play to a "third man".

A wide game does not mean playing down the wing but moving the ball from one side to the other. This is a wide game.

We should always have players (wingers and full backs) occupying the wide spaces near the flanks to use the attacking width to make the opposition's defence behave in two specific ways. The second example is on the next page.

In this example shown in the diagram, the opposition's defence stay central and close together, leaving the wide spaces open. We can occupy these spaces using our attacking width and maximise their use by moving the ball quickly across the pitch before their defensive unit can move across and/ or by creating a 2v1 situation on the flank (our winger (7) and full back (2) against one opposition defender).

Playing a 'Wide Game' to Stretch the Opposition (2)

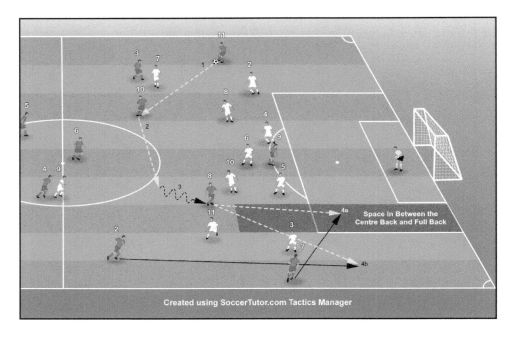

Space In Between the Centre Back and Full Back

In this second example, the opposition's defence opens up, creating space between the defenders. This does not directly favour a wide attacking game, but it does open up space inside that can be penetrated by moving the ball quickly from one side to the other and could further open the defence through attacking depth.

We can break quickly by playing one-twos and use the midfielders to penetrate the defence, (see previous examples of "Expansive Football") relating to the movement of the midfielders attacking down the centre and in other areas of the pitch.

The disorganisation and space created between the defenders is a direct result of a wide attack, as the opponents are very focused on the wide areas, so end up allowing space to open up in the centre.

We see in the diagram how the winger (7) combines with the midfielder (8) to open up a wide space for the full back to run into - marked as 'Space in Between the Centre Back and Full Back'.

The midfielder (8) with the ball has two passing options:

1. To the winger inside the penalty area (4a).

2. Out wide to the overlapping full back (4b).

The Role of the Striker

The Striker's Role in Expansive Football

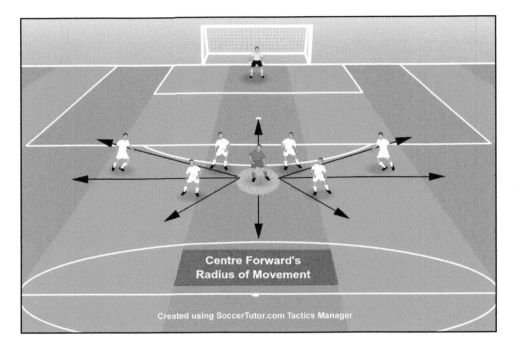

Centre Forward's Radius of Movement

Created using SoccerTutor.com Tactics Manager

Here we analyse another important aspect of "Expansive Football" - the centre forward. He should always stay high up the pitch, providing attacking depth as a spear head.

The centre forward's objectives are:

1. Create space.

2. Open up the pitch vertically (forward movement to stretch the opposition).

3. Constantly move, trying to lose his markers.

4. Be free to break into the open space in behind the defensive line.

The centre forward's radius of movement should include width as well as depth - vertically (forwards) to move directly towards the goal and horizontally to receive in behind the opponent's two defensive midfielders if they are playing with a 4-2-3-1 formation or behind the one defensive midfielder if they are playing with a 4-1-4-1.

Striker: Escaping a Marker with Unseen Movement

One movement that the centre forward should perform before he receives the ball is to "go dark" (Sans-Frattarola), looking to receive the ball in an area where his marker is unable to see both him and the ball simultaneously.

The forward should move around behind the opponent (as shown in the diagram) or look to run onto a ball played over his shoulder. It is a very useful technical-tactical skill because it frees the attacker from his marker, as shown in the diagram.

Retaining Balance in the Possession Phase

THE EFFECTIVE USE OF DRIBBLING TO DRAW MARKERS AWAY

We should not forget that dribbling is an important attacking technical action too, especially in the initiation zone (the area around the ball). There are risks, but they should be acceptable and controlled.

The centre back can dribble the ball diagonally out of defence to draw in the opponent marking the full back. When the marker is close, he then releases the pass. He can also do this if the full back is unmarked to draw the opponent away from the winger. There must always be a reason for dribbling, although the main objective is to draw a marker away from a teammate. It is more difficult to dribble once you reach the final third as there will be less space and a greater number of opposition players, but you can always do it. For example, the midfielder can dribble the ball to draw a marker away from the winger and the winger can dribble to draw his marker inside, thus creating space down the wing for the overlapping full back.

The technical action of dribbling is very important, but retention of the ball is equally as important for the team. It is a key element in a positional game as it increases player density in some areas and creates space in others.

According to Oscar Cano, retaining the ball allows for two things:

1. To draw the opposition into the space around the player with the ball to free teammates in other areas. Players must retain the ball to draw specific opponents to specific areas so teammates are free to run into space.

2. Taking time in order to give time to your teammates so that they are in their natural positions and can begin to be or continue to be dangerous.

In a 2v1 or 3v1 situation, using the midfielder -> winger -> full back combination, or when playing down the middle using the centre midfielders and striker, it is always important to make the opponents feel like they are being "attacked", thus putting them on the "defensive".

Dribbling to Draw a Marker Away and Create Space for a Teammate to Receive

Created using SoccerTutor.com Tactics Manager

In this diagram we illustrate how dribbling the ball can help the team provide balance, maintain possession and attack effectively.

When a player receives free of marking, they should make the most of the opportunity to carry the ball into the space. This action draws away one of their teammate's markers, so they can then pass to them in free space.

In the diagram above, the centre back (5) receives in space and is able to dribble at a diagonal angle towards the sideline. This draws the left back's marker (the white winger No.7) away, which enables the centre back to make an easy pass to the full back (3) in space.

The full back (3) receives in space and is able to dribble forwards. This draws the No.10's marker (the white No.8) away, which enables the full back to make an easy pass inside to him.

The attacking midfielder (10) also has space to dribble when he receives the pass. He runs with the ball at a diagonal angle and draws the left winger's marker (2) towards him. He then plays the pass to his teammate (11) who now has free space to receive on the flank and can attack in behind the opposition's defensive line.

Compensatory Movements to Provide Cover and Balance

In this example the centre back (5) is in possession and we are building up play from the back.

We want to make it clear that "compensatory movements" are very important and balance the team to make sure that the team retains its shape and there are sufficient numbers at the back in case the ball is lost.

If one full back moves forwards (the left back No.3 in the diagram example), the opposite full back (2) should stay a few yards behind, but not as deep as the centre backs.

This is very important, because if one full back goes forward, the other full back must not go too far forwards or move too far back. They must retain a balanced position in line with the defensive midfielder (6).

In this situation the centre back is free of marking so moves forwards by dribbling the ball into the midfield.

As shown in the diagram, when the centre back (5) dribbles the ball forwards into the centre, the defensive midfielder (6) should move back to provide balance. The two players interchange positions.

Retaining a Balanced Formation in the Possession Phase

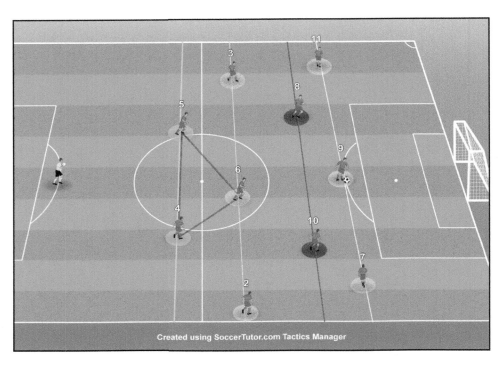

Created using SoccerTutor.com Tactics Manager

In the diagram above we look at the formation (team shape) that we aim to achieve when in possession in the attacking phase. This set up allows the players to be in positions to support each other, for the team to retain balance and to prepare for the transition from attack to defence.

In this example the striker is in possession high up the pitch and the attacking 4-3-3 formation has transformed into a 2-3-2-3. The diagram shows the players in lines, however as shown on the previous page, the players will often interchange positions using "compensatory movements".

We should always maintain a defensive triangle (marked in red in the diagram) behind

the ball using the two centre backs and the defensive midfielder in the positions shown. They can interchange positions when necessary.

The full backs (2 and 3) are in the same line as the defensive midfielder, however one full back can move forwards to join the attack (as shown on the previous page), but the other full back must make sure to stay back.

The two attacking midfielders (8 and 10) are a step higher up the pitch. The striker (9) and the wingers (7 and 11) are a few yards higher up than them.

Intervention, Phase and Cooperation Spaces

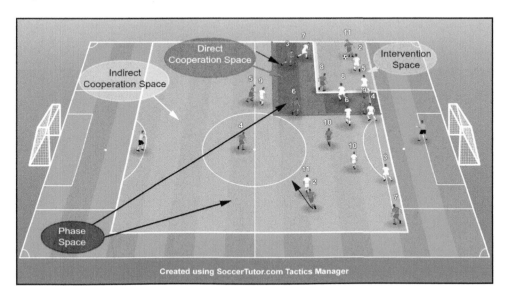

Created using SoccerTutor.com Tactics Manager

It is very important to define the zones on the pitch so that the players know how to interpret them correctly. In this example, the winger (11) is in possession high up the pitch and we have marked out the zones according to this situation.

When in the possession phase we have 2 zones:

1. *"Intervention Space"* (YELLOW)

This is the zone where the ball is (yellow area highlighted in the diagram).

2. *"Phase Space"* (WHITE + RED)

The rest of the pitch is all part of the "phase space". Within the phase spaces, the other players directly combine with the player (No.11 in the diagram) inside the intervention space.

Within the phase space we have 2 zones:

2a. *"Indirect Cooperation Space"* (WHITE)

This area is highlighted in white and is occupied by the players furthest from the intervention space who perform compensatory movements to provide balance. The diagram shows that when one full back (3) goes forwards, the other full back (2) moves back. The defensive midfielder is always in a covering position.

2b. *"Direct Cooperation Space"* (RED)

This area is highlighted in red and is occupied by the players directly supporting the players in the intervention space. In the diagram we show the left back (3) who has moved forwards, the attacking midfielder (8) and the striker (9) all in support within the direct cooperation space.

Providing Support and Maintaining Defensive Shape in Possession

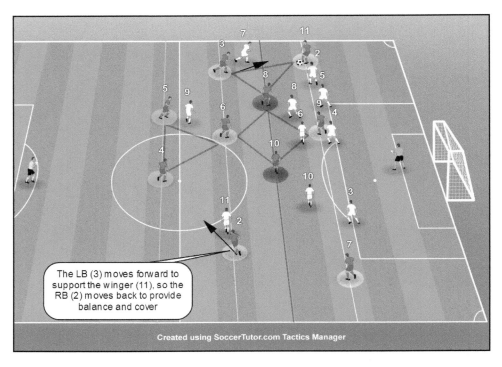

The LB (3) moves forward to support the winger (11), so the RB (2) moves back to provide balance and cover

Created using SoccerTutor.com Tactics Manager

In the diagram above we have again highlighted the team shape when in possession. The formation changes from a 4-3-3 to a 2-3-2-3 with 4 lines. This is very important for two different reasons:

1. We will always have players available to support an attack, playing with triangles or rhombus shapes (shown in red).

2. There are four lines of depth defensively, as shown in the diagram.

Playing in this way, we occupy the whole pitch and allow the compensatory movements of the defensive midfielder and the full backs, which were explained on the previous pages.

It is important that the players, and especially the full backs push up in our "Expansive

Football" attack. They stay at the same height as the defensive midfielder (6), so that they have less ground to cover than if they were level with the centre backs. If the full backs play in line with the centre backs, they will be too far away to support in the attacking phase. If we lose the ball they will obviously have further to track back, but not much further. By playing in this way they will be close to the centre of the game, or "intervention space" (explained on previous page).

When the winger has the ball (11), the full back (3) moves up to create a numerical superiority not only in the attacking phase, but also in case of a transition from attack to defence. If we lose the ball many of our players are close by to help win it back quickly.

The Transition from Attack to Defence

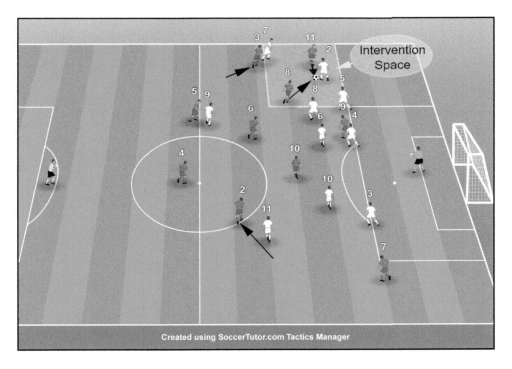

Here we have the same situation as on the previous pages with the winger (11) in possession high up the pitch.

The winger loses the ball to the opposition's right back (2).

The winger (11) is the first player to apply pressure to the new ball carrier within the "Intervention Space" with the support of the attacking midfielder (8) - double marking to win the ball back as quickly as possible.

The left back (3) who had moved forwards is then able to step up and mark the white No.7 (a potential receiver of the next pass) tightly - fencing him in.

The defensive midfielder (6) and the full back (2) on the other side of the pitch provide balance for the team in case the whites are able to break through the pressure and launch an attack.

COHESION BETWEEN DYNAMIC SPACES

Dynamic spaces are not zones or fixed areas, but are dynamic and continually moving and mutating. They depend on all of the players of both teams as the reference and as a consequence are not "closed" but "open" spaces where uncertainty reigns.

It is important to repeat that we must concentrate enough players in the intervention and direct support spaces thinking not only of attack, but of defence as well. The game phases cannot be separated and how you attack and defend are not interdependent of each other.

Football, as Manuel Conde states, must be trained as a whole. Therefore we must form a positional combination attack by concentrating many players in the intervention space providing mutual support.

As we have said before, with the defensive objective of recovering the ball and playing a good transitional game when progressing closer to the opposition's goal, if the ball is not recovered quickly, we move into an effective defensive phase creating a compact defensive block with very narrow and reduced vertical/ horizontal spaces.

By placing a large number of players in the intervention and direct support spaces we create a numerical superiority in defence, with players moving towards the ball and thus limiting the time and space that the opponents have. By closing them down quickly they have less time to analyse the situation and less space to move the ball about. We only achieve this by being together in attack and not too dispersed. Separated yes, but within the optimal distance so that we can separate the opposition.

We must not leave players isolated and unable to act, whether in attack, defence or the transitional phases. When we lose the ball all of our players should move closer together and closer to their nearest opponent so that the opponent highest up the pitch can be played offside.

As Pep Guardiola says, *"We pass backwards to attack and pass forwards to defend".*

So, in summary, we must attack and defend as one, maintaining tight lines and performing as a functional unit.

The Importance of Cohesion to Prevent Isolating One Player

After a long pass, the left back steals the ball. We are too far away to press, so the opposition counter attack

Created using SoccerTutor.com Tactics Manager

We do not play many long, high passes so as not to isolate a player. It is preferable to always have a numerical superiority around the ball. If the attacking midfielders or defensive midfielder always play a long pass out to the winger, then the winger will often find himself in a 1v1 situation.

If the opponent wins the ball and moves forwards our players will be too far apart to apply pressure and will be too far from the intervention space and, therefore, the ball. The opposition can easily counter attack in that situation.

This very important concept is demonstrated in the diagram above:

CHAPTER 3

METHODOLOGIES TO USE IN TRAINING

METHODOLOGIES TO USE IN TRAINING

You need a method and a methodology to perform any type of activity. Currently in Spain, three working methodologies prevail:

1. ATR (accumulation, transformation & realisation)

2. Tactical periodization

3. Structured approach

ATR focuses on the physical workload of accumulation, transformation and realisation and has its roots in traditional athletic theories based on workload etc.

So instead, we will focus on the other two methodologies that have a 'systemic' base. This term has its basis in the fact that football is a system, a set of elements that interact with each other within a context and towards a common goal. They act as a network, one small change in any element influences the other members. This theory is the scientific basis of tactical periodization and the structured approach.

TACTICAL PERIODIZATION

"Tactical Periodization" is a systematic training methodology based on the game model that the coach wants his team to apply, the periodization of the games principles and sub-principles. The game model is the game that the coach wants his team to play together within a context such as the characteristics of the club, the players, the country's culture etc.

Tactical Periodization is based on these fundamental principals:

- *Principle of Specificity*: All work is based on the game model that we follow.

- *Repetition Principle:* Repetition of what we

want to work on within a contextualised drill. The systematic repetition of actions to create habits, the "Expertise within the expertise".

- *Complex Progression Principle:* Prioritise and give a hierarchy to the principles and sub-principles moving from the less complex to the complex. This principle controls the complexity of the exercises to make sure that the players arrive in the best possible condition on match day and that there is always acquisition.

- *Horizontal Rotation Principle:* Alternate the tension, duration and the speed of the specific muscular contractions. It does not create peaks in form going from training session to training session instead of drill to drill.

- *Psychological/Physical Intensity Principle:* As Santos and Pinehiro say, this is a fundamental training parameter. It refers more to cognitive intensity than physical intensity. This emotional intensity must be integrated into the drills according to the period of the micro-cycle that we are in. The exercises (regardless of the objective and game model) develop and maintain the players in the maximum psychological/physical state to adapt the body to real game situations. This means that each training session (especially in the week before a game) should have an emotional charge similar to that of a competitive game. Each session should be of high concentration and high intensity with a similar duration to an actual game, about 90-100 minutes.

Then, to carry out the game model we must structure some game principles and sub-principles. The principles will be the general behaviours the coach wants to see from his

team. The sub-principles are more specific behaviours found within these general behaviours.

There are a series of principles, so called fundamental principles, that the team must always follow, whether that is the game model, system or formation. What should happen if, for example, a centre back moves out to intercept a ball? His teammates in the defensive line should close the space behind him. There should always be a defensive line of 4 or 5 players regardless of what system is being played.

We then have the general principles of our game model which also vary according to the system, e.g. The type of attack. In this book we will work on our "Expansive Football" positional attack so one of the principles would be width in attack by all players. A sub-principle would be that the wingers and the full backs open up the pitch and do not play in line with the centre midfielders, so that there are open passing channels.

THE STRUCTURED APPROACH

This leads on to Seirul.lo's methodology, the "Structured Focus". This is structured with a systematic basis, but does not have the same tactical influences as tactical periodization. This methodology considers the players as a series of structures that interact with each other, creating synergies within a context.

These structures are:

- *Cognitive (decision making):* The players' perception of tactical situations and the appropriate solutions.

- *Conditioning:* Physical fitness and strength to provide support and resolve situations.

- *Coordination:* Technical actions, motor skills.

- *Social Effectiveness:* The relationship between the player and his teammates.

- *The Work Ethic and Motivation:* The willingness of the player to work, train, play and identify with the team.

- *Creative/Expressive:* Take the "I" from the player. Use all that he knows, his originality, innate and learned creativity to resolve this situation.

Following this methodology the player will develop all of the structures that he needs to interact with his teammates. This is only possible if we apply PSS (Preferred Simulated Situations). As Juanma Lillo says, *"The drills are situations and should have those characteristics".* They should simulate real game situations which are denaturalised and respect specific temporal and spatial tactics. They are preferred because they prioritise some structures over others.

We see that there is not much social-affectivity between the players so we create social effective drills, such as a circular drill similar to piggy in the middle but instead of the player in the middle being the player who lost the ball, it can be the player who made the last pass or a player who is not in the correct position to receive the ball.

It is vital that the player knows what he needs to prioritise within each drill so that he can focus his attention and concentrate on it, whilst also taking everything else into account. The players should become aware of which are the preferred collective behaviours and what we are looking for and the drills should be repeated, systemising those behaviours through training.

According to this methodology (Albert Roca and Agustín Lleida) the situations could be:

- *General:* The nature and organisation are less than that seen in competition and decision making is zero, such as interval training.

- *Directed:* There is a ball but no specific decision making nor opposition, such as a passing combination.

- *Specific:* There is a ball and opposition with specific decision making but the format is not the same as a real game, such as a 4v2 drill.

- *Competitive:* with all of the ingredients of a simulated game with some competitiveness.

There are two principles of this methodology that we want to highlight:

1.   **The Complementarity Principle, of Oscar Cano:**

     Before we used players who compensated for each other, such as using one attacking and one defensive player in centre midfield, or having one centre back who was tall and strong paired with one smaller and faster. That is no longer the case. Barcelona use players with the same characteristics, that have, as they say in Italy, "good feet", meaning that they know how to play football and create effective group associations, aligning players who can play together the most effectively.

2.   **Prospective Power Principle:**

     The ability of the player to resolve situations differently so that they are not predictable. The situations and drills have to have this variety, with a repetition of different solutions to these situations.

     In this book, which will be somewhat contradictory, we will mix these two streams to create a session and a series of drills in order to work on "Expansive Football". As you will see it is a little eclectic. So, let's get down to business!

CHAPTER 4

THE SOCIAL-AFFECTIVE DIMENSION (TEAMWORK AND COLLABORATION)

THE SOCIAL AFFECTIVE DIMENSION

We consider the social-affective dimension as one of the most influential aspects for any team. The associations created between players are vital to a team. The resulting interactions distinguish one squad from another (collectively not individually). The idea that one player can win you a game is an important one, but it is the team that will win you a Championship. Relationships between the players depend on the context as they are influenced by many things, such as their opponents, refereeing decisions and the supporters. In addition, there are personal factors that can influence a footballer, like his mood or personal relationships off the pitch with his partner, family etc.

These influences create these variables; tactical (referring to the game itself, teammates, opponents etc.) and human (referring to the player as a human and not a robot). The player should see himself as "Me plus" all of the previously mentioned variables, although not in an isolated way, but as part of a group, which is why we used the word "plus".

A team is made up of several collective structures based on individual ones, which are:

- **TACTICAL**
- **TECHNICAL**
- **PHYSICAL**
- **MENTAL AND CULTURAL**

By cultural we mean that the players have a wealth of solutions when faced with situations that occur on the pitch. Barcelona players are taught that tactical culture from an early age. We need to ensure that the players in our team have a similar tactical culture. It is a team when all of the players will choose the same solution when faced with the same situation.

These structures and their relationship give

meaning to the associations of the players and always emphasise that the aim of the game is not only individual but collective, so that the players must play for their team considering these structures and the given context. This means not simply looking to retrieve the ball, but to look at the situation and see how it can be resolved with a clear objective, thus positively helping the team. These structures and their interrelation should be related at the same time to the variables, "Me plus…".

These relationships between players create interdependencies that are very important in helping the team to grow. If each player improves through the associations and synergies then everyone will improve, as will the team.

Everything a player does should make sense to the subsequent move. A good pass allows a teammate to play a quick one-two with another teammate, so he should not need to control the ball, but instead be well placed to play one touch football, providing rhythm to the game, and so on down the chain.

Chema Sanz, the excellent fitness coach told us, *"In a good team, all of the players should cooperate with each other harmoniously in order to benefit the team even though each player has his own possibilities. We are people in situations and our capabilities depend on who we are and what surrounds us".* We must highlight the phrase, *"We are all people in situations"*, as sometimes we forget that footballers are not robots, but are human and can make mistakes. It is alright if a player makes a mistake if he learns from it and improves.

Our teams must follow Lotina's idea that we should not only want very good players, but they should also be very good at playing together.

The relationships and interactions between players can have a huge influence. With this in mind we offer the humble opinion that Messi is not "the same Messi" with Argentina as he is with Barcelona. And was it the same Kaka that played for Milan and Real Madrid? This has happened plenty of times, a player has a fantastic season and moves on to a better team only to end up on the bench.

The social-affective relationships influence the associations within a team as much or more than tactics. When we talk about the social-affective dimension we are referring to the work ethic of the team to cooperate and attack together (good passes, making yourself available for a pass, creating space for a teammate etc.) and cooperate defensively (pressing, closing down space, covering and exchanging positions etc.).

The social-affective dimension would therefore be the spirit of the team found in all technical-tactical actions both attacking and defending. For example, covering a teammate in defence to help him against an opponent, helping double up or covering a position are all tactical defensive actions full of social effectivity: *"I will defend my teammate from an attack".* You also see it in attacking moves in the cooperation between the players with their movement. For example, an attacking player helps his teammate lose his marker and creates space that can be occupied by a striker making a deep run, or a winger comes inside and the full back overlaps. All are examples of the social-affective dimension.

COLLABORATION OF MOVEMENT

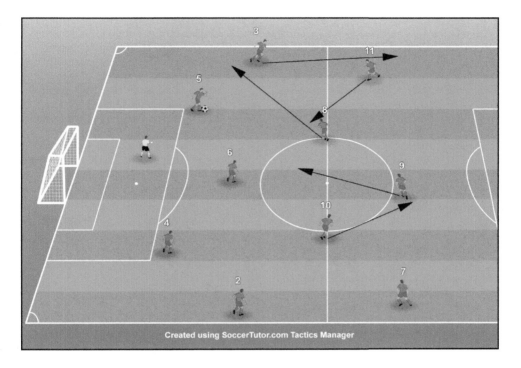

Created using SoccerTutor.com Tactics Manager

If you look at the diagram above you can see these interesting movements and a great deal of collaboration. For example, when the centre back (5) has the ball, the striker (9) goes to support him and No.10 moves into his space. The attacking midfielder No.8 moves into the space left by the full back (3) who has moved forward into the winger's (11) position. No.11 had moved into the space that No.8 left.

We see that there has to be a great deal of cooperation between the players, offering multiple solutions to the player with the ball. They are in continuous motion, together and in unison to help the player with the ball at all times.

THE RESPONSIBILITIES OF THE COACH

The coach should be very open to creating good relationships and synergies between the players, not only from a tactical and strategical point of view but he should stimulate and reinforce their sense of unity, not just the tactical interdependency but the team spirit. The coach must know how to generate positive emotions in his players. The player should cooperate and collaborate with his teammates tactically and with spirit in order to win the game. This is what a team is; having a common objective and the knowledge that they can only achieve it together.

The more you work on the "spiritual" aspect of the team, the easier the tactical work will become. There will be more union and accomplishment. Covering, for example, will have a very strong significance, knowing how important it is to protect your teammate or knowing that a space that you have opened up will be occupied by an overlapping player is very rewarding.

NON VERBAL COMMUNICATION

We should mention that communication between the players is vital and is mainly non-verbal. Their movement speaks and transmits different information. The social skills of communication, assertiveness and empathy permanently flourish within a team full of social-affectivity, continuously feeding off itself and strengthening the ties that bind the players. It is therefore very important that the players learn to understand and learn how to interpret what their teammate wants to say through his movement. It creates a language, a movement code that only they know how to understand and interpret.

The coach should be capable of developing within his team the concept of assertive motor skills through training drills. This means that the player gives the correct response to his teammate through his movement, helping him to solve the situation efficiently and correctly. If, for example, the player with the ball needs his teammate's help, the teammate uses a specific type of movement, loses his marker and makes himself available for a pass. With a mutual understanding, the receiver knows that the only solution is to position himself in a certain way to enable the player in possession to pass him the ball and thus provide continuity.

To sum up, the player in possession and possible and probable receivers of the ball are continuously sending messages through their movement and they must collectively learn to decode the messages and be completely in tune with each other.

Therefore it is important that real game situations are repeatedly simulated during training so that they can be recognised and interpreted by all of the players. It is vital that there are open situations so that the players can communicate freely using their assertive motor skills.

EMOTION AND EMPATHY

Emotion is very important in assertive motor communication and influences it enormously. The player must want to understand his teammate and help him in his current situation. Empathy and knowing where to be on the pitch helps decipher and understand what the players want to say. The more emotion you feel towards your teammates the more you will want to help them and understand them in order to provide them with a solution.

COACHING STAFF AND PLAYER RELATIONSHIPS

We must stress that the social-affectivity should not only be between the players, but must also occur between the coaches and their staff. The coaches must have socio-affectivity with their players so that they can understand them, be understood and get the most out of them. If the players see, notice and feel this affection from the coach it will be reciprocated. We know that when a player does not play he usually blames the coach but if we can promote bidirectional affectivity (capability of reacting or functioning in two different ways) then the player will think that it is not the managers fault that he is not playing as he has demonstrated that he only wants the best for him, but it will be because he has not trained well and he will apply himself more.

Social-affectivity is fostered not only through words but through actions, facts and empathy. We have several examples of where Guardiola and Mourinho have demonstrated this. When he was at Barcelona, Guardiola cancelled a training session so that the entire team of players and back room staff could go to the funeral of the father of one of the staff. Another famous example was when a well known automobile company gifted cars to each of the players and to Guardiola himself. Guardiola refused to accept his as cars were not given to the rest of the back room staff. Mourinho always refers to his team and back room staff as "family", as a unique family that should be united in the face of adversity.

When you create these emotional ties they emerge and manifest themselves when faced with different situations causing a very strong emotion. This year at Bayern Munich for example, a young player called Höjbjerg went to Guardiola heartbroken to tell him that his father was very ill with cancer. Guardiola hugged him and cried with him and then made sure that the club did everything in its power to help the players father.

Mourinho gave us another example of the strong emotional connection a manger can have with his players when he won the European Cup with Inter. He bumped into Materazzi in the car park afterwards and the two of them embraced and cried silently together for several minutes without uttering a word.

HOW TO CREATE STRONG TEAM EMOTIONS

The coach should therefore stimulate the emotions within and outside the training sessions between himself and the players. *"Together we form a team."* Going back to training, you can use powerful phrases to help convey this feeling, and to promote team spirit.

Some powerful phrases would be:

- *"When they kick your teammate, that kick has to hurt us all"* (Unai Emery)

- *"If one walks, there are 10 who suffer, we will not allow it because we are a team"* (Jorge D'Alessandro)

- *"The moment you stop fighting, you've lost the sense of being a team."*

These statements should be inserted in preferred simulated situations. There are many social-affective drills. All drills/practices that use 2 or more players, whether attacking or defending, have social-affective elements.

Social-Affective Practices (Teamwork and Collaboration)

Aerial Control and Shooting Practice in a Dynamic 2 v 2 Game

Objective

To practice aerial passing, control, shooting and 2v2 play. There is a lot of social-affectivity (teamwork and collaboration) in this drill both in attack (overlapping, one-twos etc.) and in defence (covering, interchanging of positions etc.).

Description

We can play a 2v2 game in an area double the size of the penalty box, with 4 teams in total.

We start with a normal 2v2 game. The first pair to score a goal stays in the game.

When they score they move closer to the other goal (as shown in the phase 2 diagram) and a rival player on the outside plays in a high pass for one of them to play a controlled pass (one touch pass) straight to their partner. It must be a good touch so that his partner can control it easily and immediately attack.

After the second phase is finished, the 2 pairs swap with the outside pairs and we continue.

Coaching Points

The player receiving the ball after the long pass must position himself well and be in line with the player passing him the ball, as shown in the diagram.

Teamwork in a Dynamic Positional 4 v 4 Small Sided Game

Objective

To develop positional play, teamwork and communication in a competitive 4v4 game.

Description

In the same area as the previous practice (double the size of the penalty box), we play 4v4 with an extra neutral player (yellow). The basis of the game is normal with both teams able to score. The neutral player plays with the team in possession but is not allowed to score.

We start the practice with a 4v1 (+1 neutral player). The defensive player (white) will struggle against 5 opponents but he has teammates who will help him. Every 10 seconds one of his teammates joins the game until all 4 have entered creating a 5v4 situation.

If the whites win the ball, they launch a counter attack and try to score.

Variation

Instead of the teammates making a timed entrance and, to make the drill more about teamwork and collaboration, they can work for it. The players waiting to enter can perform 30 sit-ups and are then allowed to enter the game when they have completed them. This way the players must perform them quickly in order to help their teammates.

Teamwork and Collaboration in a 4 v 2 Possession Game

Created using SoccerTutor.com Tactics Manager

Objective

To develop positional play, teamwork and communication in a possession game.

Description

In a 10 x 10 yard area, we play a 4v2 possession game. We have 4 players on the outside and 2 players in the middle. The aim for the 4 players is to maintain possession, making sure to use good collaboration of movement and communication. They are limited to 1 or 2 touches.

The 2 defenders work together to close the passing angles and press the ball to win it.

Coaching Point

Usually, the player in the middle is the player who lost the ball but that is not so in a socio-affective practice because there may have been various reasons why he lost the ball. The judgment in this practice should be different because maybe a teammate was not in the correct position to receive the pass or he received a bad pass from another teammate.

Teamwork and Collaboration in a Dynamic 3 Pairs Possession Game

After intercepting; pass to teammate before moving to outside

Ball intercepted; the teammate of the player who lost the ball closes down the new ball carrier

Created using SoccerTutor.com Tactics Manager

Objective

To develop positional play, teamwork and communication in a possession game.

Description

This is a slight variation of the previous practice and is another type of socio-affective possession game (4v2 in pairs). When a middle player (whites in diagram) wins the ball he should try to pass it to his partner, while the teammate of the player who lost the ball aggressively closes him down to stop him playing the pass. This is a highly socio-affective drill.

The player that wins the ball needs to quickly be in the correct position to make the pass and avoid being pressured by the teammate of the player who lost the ball (red) who is looking to tackle or intercept the pass. If the pass is successfully made, the pair in the middle (whites) can pass to the blues. The whites and reds swap roles and the practice continues.

Variations

All of these 4 practices can be adapted by changing the size of the playing area, time and number of players involved. For example, instead of playing 2v2 or 4v2, you can change it to 3v3 or 6v3, making sure you always follow the principles of our game model.

CHAPTER 5

THE EMOTIONAL WILL DIMENSION (COMPETITIVENESS AND DESIRE TO WIN)

THE EMOTIONAL WILL DIMENSION

This dimension, as with the previous one, is very important because it is the difference between feeling like winners and feeling beaten. The emotional will sphere is the feeling of competitiveness, the immense desire to do well. When two teams have the same quality, technique, tactics and strength, this is what makes the difference, formed by pride and will. This is what makes a player want to be the best, the champion. If he unites this with the social-affective dimension then, with the help of his teammates, he can achieve it. This is a team!

The coach must ensure that each player has this will, this desire inside them to succeed. Albert Einstein said that, *"the most powerful force is not nuclear or electricity, it is the human will."* To work on this area the coach should encourage self-confidence, will, determination and perseverance in achieving the objective of the exercises, for both attacking and defending. The player has to learn to adapt to uncertain situations and seek continuous improvement in quality, competitive spirit and sacrifice, understanding that the prize will be worth it. Success will be the reward for all the efforts made and sustained. In short, do not lose sight of this vision.

The coach must make the player mentally strong, able to fight frustration, to be pro-active, resilient and a resonant leader.

By competitive situations we refer to those practices in which the player has to compete to win. There are rivals who also want to win. You want them not only to win, but to outdo themselves too. You not only need to focus on the exercise itself, but on the rules and the ultimate goal. For example, in a 2v2 socio-affective practice, you can prioritise the emotional will sphere by saying that the team who wins more games will be the best, so in the end they can take a few extra penalties or remove the goalkeeper, or not have to perform extra sit-ups etc. Encourage the competitive spirit, winning achieves a prize that only they can have.

Practices that encourage competition and cooperation, such as 2v1 or 2v2 are very important. Avoid 1v1 drills as there is no socio-affectivity, no team spirit like you find in a 2v2 or 2v1. The teammate helps his partner to be better. There are thousands of competitive practices of varying complexity, from scoring more to staying in the opponent's half.

HOW THIS IS ACHIEVED

We must create practices that represent competitive situations and by knowing how to transmit the necessary information to make the players feel and understand this emotional will dimension.

Emotional Will (Desire to Win) Practice Example

Description

In this practice example, we position 2 pairs as shown in the diagram. Allocate the pairs in relation to their playing position. In the diagram example, we have 2 centre backs (red) and 2 attackers (white).

There is a ball in the middle and the players set off at the same time. The pair that gets to the ball first takes possession and can combine to attack and try to score past the goalkeeper. The other pair defends so that all of the areas are being worked on:

- **Tactics** (Link play, looking for attacking and defensive solutions.)
- **Socio-affective** (Cooperation in attack/defence, technique, encouraging competitiveness and the desire to reach the ball before the opponent in order to be the attackers. It is always more stimulating to be on the attack as there is a tangible reward - to win.)

Coaching Points

1. The attacking pair should use one-two's, vertical passes and overlapping runs.
2. The defending pair should interchange positions, block passes and cover each other.

PSYCHOLOGICAL TECHNIQUES

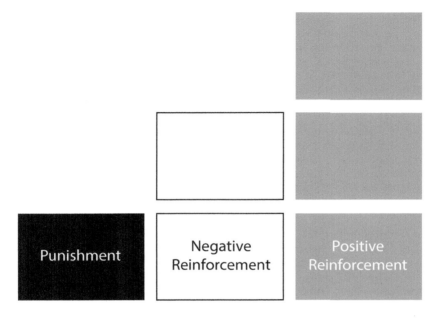

Punishment

Negative
Reinforcement

Positive
Reinforcement

When we correct behaviour we are stimulating the emotional will sphere at the same time. If a player sees that he is doing well, receiving awards and positive rewards for his actions, that dimension will increase more and more. There are many types of ways to develop the emotional will dimension with psychological techniques. Here are three we consider very useful and effective for correct behaviour:

1. POSITIVE REINFORCEMENT

2. NEGATIVE REINFORCEMENT

3. PUNISHMENT

As José Maria Buceta says, positive reinforcement would be to apply a positive stimulus as a result of conduct that is intended to strengthen, thus making sure that this behaviour will occur again. For example, the coach effusively praises the player that has passed the ball to the right, when he came

from the left, as expressed in the "Expansive Football" model and through encouragement this behaviour will be repeated.

Negative reinforcement, as stated by Jose Maria Buceta, removes a negative stimulus as a result of the conduct that is to be strengthened, making such behaviour more likely. For example, following the example above, we want the player to collect the ball from one side and move it to another. However, a player who does not perform this action very well gets told off as a consequence.

Punishment would be to apply a negative stimulus so that a certain behaviour is not repeated. Following the "Expansive Football" model, when we do not want a player to repeat a certain action, for example, rather than spreading the ball wide he repeatedly returns it to the player that passed it to him,

the punishment could be to collect up the equipment at the end of the session.

Social reinforcement is also very important and very useful and consists of publicly praising behaviours that are repeated with words, gestures or the universal "OK" sign. Approval of positive conduct feeds the emotional will dimension. Be careful that you do not only give praise as you could lose credibility. To be able to educate you must also be able to say no and not tolerate bad or incorrect behaviours.

The emotional will sphere, i.e. Intentionality and the desire to want to do things right, is a behaviour and as such should be strengthened. It is important that we always try to apply positive reinforcement and to a lesser extent, negative reinforcement. We rarely use punishment.

It is important to apply the reinforcement appropriately, according to the moment, situation and person. All of the players are people first, then footballers so you must find the most appropriate punishment for each. Our experience tells us that positive and social reinforcements are very effective for everyone.

REAL LIFE EXAMPLES

I once read a newspaper story about a team in Scotland who used a method of punishment that consisted of making the player who had put the least effort into training all week wear a different colour bib during the warm up before the weekend game. The player had to wear the bib for all of the warm up drills as a symbol of his "laziness". As a result, the players all trained very hard so that they did not have to wear it and be singled out as players who did not give their very best as obviously they would have to wear the bib not only in front of their teammates but also the media and fans.

One day I took this punishment and I transformed it into positive reinforcement. The pair or trio in any link of the chain (also promoting socio-affectivity and tactics) that had trained better than their teammates during the week would wear different coloured bibs as a symbol of their great self-sacrifice and good work as role models. We had a press conference almost every week and those players would be the ones I took to be interviewed. Promoting the emotional will sphere in this way, the players trained hard not only to win but to be the best. This technique worked wonders.

INFLUENCE OF THE COACH

It is not only the practices that influence this sphere but the work of the coach. As my friend and fellow coach, Eloi Martinez says, *"We should always be on top of the players, stimulating them and motivating them to win".* And why not? Why not nip at them to get the best out of them? And reminding them of the importance of work and the consequences of doing it correctly; the prize. Being on top of them does not mean treating them badly or overwhelming them because we are all people after all, it simply means pushing them positively towards success.

Footballers and people in general, work much better when they are feeling positive emotions and have stimuli that invoke positive reactions. We should make most situations positive and keep the players animated. Guardiola said it best, *"When my players do not play well I do not fight them but encourage them".*

The coach has to squeeze a lot out of his players and they should be aware of his presence. He should be able to motivate as well as give instructions and merely be a technical guide. It is not good enough to simply say "come on, come on, come on"; the verbal language and stimulating phrases should be accompanied by body language (applauding, high fives, making the "OK" sign and all of the social reinforcements that we have referred to before). We need to make the

players feel the importance of the emotional will dimension.

A run of losing games can influence the emotional will sphere. I came to the conclusion that my players not only lacked confidence in themselves but that they were also missing an internal and group leader, a resounding leader. I wanted them to understand that if they struggled, fought and were determined to play well in order to win then their inner leader would come out and it would draw out the leadership qualities in their teammates.

I directed the exercise towards letting the player discover his own quality and potential, touching his pride and letting his self emerge.

I focused the instructions on "valour" using phrases such as **"A win today means more than 3 points"**. Keep the focus on what you want to achieve and win this season and emphasise that people can no longer live in their glorious past but must bring out the great players that they are inside and play for him and for the team. Compare the opposition to a fortress or castle (a similar idea to that of Massimo de Paoli) that should be attacked. Develop their feelings of love for themselves, their self esteem and pride, making them believe that they are "the kings of their castles" which must be defended tooth and nail (referring to the team's defensive unit). At the same time they must be brave, attacking the enemy castle to conquer it (the opposition's defensive unit). The players identified with this concept and with this sense of identity.

Sometimes I spoke about their families; wives, parents and children. I spoke about the importance of winning for them, to dedicate their victories to them, all of which motivated the players. Once, before the last game of the season (which we needed to win to be promoted), I brought all of the players families into the changing room and said "You must win for all of us". Together, in a changing room packed with players, parents, wives and children, we let out a "battle cry" which released an explosion of adrenaline. Paco

Jimenez did a similar thing last year with Rayo Vallecano.

Here are some emotional will and socio-affective phrases:

- *"We play as we live, as we are, we want the ball, we want to attack, we want to be leaders, take risks or, if we need to, we will change and behave how we are not: we will close up the back and play long balls if that is what gets us to the enemies castle in their absence, like thieves".*

- *"I am....us".*

- *"In life, we have objectives and send ourselves, or we give our objectives to others and become their slaves".*

- *"What can we do together so that each expresses his maximum potential?" (Oscar Cano).*

- *"As a team we have a common goal which we can only achieve together".*

- *"Individually we are waves, together we are the ocean".*

- *"Everything that we give to the team will come back to us tenfold".*

CHAPTER 6

THE BASE THAT SUPPORTS THE GAME MODEL

THE BASE THAT SUPPORTS THE GAME MODEL

Through the interactions between the players, the coach helps the players to identify

What they are

How they can develop

What they can grow to be

A game model is fundamental for every team. It is the map that helps you reach your goal, your guide so that you don't get lost. Each coach should have his tactical game model which should be carefully expanded upon depending on the players that he has at his disposal, his coaching staff and the synergies and relationships that these footballers have with each other.

VISION AND FULFILLING POTENTIAL

Let the players grow. Above everything else, this is the primary basis of the game model. This is why a game model that makes one team triumphant does not guarantee success for another team as the players and contexts are different. We repeat that it is vital for each coach to have a game model to guide all training processes and the game model should be subject to continuous change and evolution. Why? Because the team is constantly changing and evolving because it is a living thing. Even with the same players,

a team's tactical model will change from one season to the next as we should be changing and adapting it continually.

The footballers and their relationships and interactions with the coaching team make the game model. It is what they carry inside. You must start from there, from what they are, and direct them towards what they can become, not in an isolated way but together. It is therefore very important that the coach helps them to help themselves through the training processes he devises. Through their interactions they must recognise what they are, what they have been, what they can achieve and what they can become.

RELATIONSHIPS BETWEEN PLAYERS

Arsenal manager Arsene Wenger said it well, *"A team is only as strong as the relationships between its players".*

The interactions make the difference, they are the pieces of the puzzle that need to be

put together. How often has a coach taken a team's star player with him when he has moved to a new club? Often, the player ends up unneeded and on the bench. It's not because he isn't a world class player but because he has not adapted to the new interactions with his new teammates. As Alberto González says, *"The game model is not the result of a sum of each players actions but the interactions that emerge between all of them".*

So, to create a game model for a team you must know the players within the team and the relationships and interactions between them. You must know what will happen if you mix the team a certain way and what will happen if you mix them in a different way. We must also take into account our reality; the context, the club itself, the history, the objectives and the football culture. The game model that we apply to Barcelona will be different to that of another club with a different reality.

It is clear that first and foremost we, as coaches, need to know the football, the game itself. We need to recognise its logic.

We must not forget that we too have our own natures, our own way of being, but we must try to connect that with the natures of the footballers that we train. We may have a tendency towards playing one style or another of football but we must adapt and be in symphony with the players. The players do not have to move towards you nor you towards them but you should all meet in the middle and go in harmony.

The nature of the players as a result of the interactions should be related to the nature of the coach. National teams are a very clear example of this. How many national teams take blocks of players from specific teams? Take for example the Spanish National team that won two European Championship (2008 and 2012) and the World Cup (2010). The large majority of the players were from Barcelona and the team was filled up of players with similar characteristics. Look at the Italian team

at the World Cup in 1994 when nearly all of their players came from Milan. They do not only assemble very good players from winning teams but, more importantly, they understand perfectly how to play together. If you look closely at both teams, the managers were in perfect symphony with those players and with their style of play; Vicente Del Bosque with Spain and Arrigo Sacchi with Italy.

The relationships between the players and the coach are fundamental. It goes further than simply an affinity to the style or method of play. For all that we know about football and coaches, how many elite coaches managing teams full of highly talented players with similar playing styles have failed because they do not have this harmony with the players and staff, this chemistry, this feeling? We do not wish to be negative, in fact we want to be the opposite and rejoice in the magic of football! How do we have this chemistry between the context, players and coach? This unity, this communion, this love at first sight? We can read as many books as we like, know all that we can about psychology and coaching but we will never know how to get that chemistry, and perhaps it is better that way.

MATCHING THE STYLE TO THE PLAYERS

A good coach should master all of the styles of play although we will always favour a specific one. You see it very clearly with the elite teams, with all of the coaches who tread water every year in the top flight. The coach can know everything in the world about football but their team does not perform, not because they are unprepared, capable or highly competent, but because their preferred style of football does not suit the club.

We repeat, the players and their character are the starting point. As Oscar Cano said, *"We must start with the player and then the type of game that they are capable of playing. The*

players take this to the training ground to generate this cycle of growth; who I am, who we are, how we can play. This should be taken into every training session".

You must "let the players be", and hold them responsible to what they are and what they can grow to be and achieve.

THE IMPORTANCE OF TACTICS

Remember that it is vital to know the game, specifically tactics. The game model should have tactics as the principal guide in order for the players to grow.

When you read an interview with a coach in any football magazine they are always asked, "what is never missing from your training sessions?" They usually reply, "the ball", but we would say, "tactics!" Individual and team attacking and defensive tactics. They can start by being analysed but aimed towards a specific decision making process (you must learn to drive on a closed circuit before they let you head into town) so that they later take a more structured route.

So, "Expansive football" is an idea of the game in the attacking phase. We refer to it as the type of football coaches have in mind for this phase (resulting from the observation of the characters of the players and relationships between them) and what we would like our team to do. In a nutshell, it is a conception of the game.

GAME MODEL FOR MAJOR PRINCIPLES AND SUB PRINCIPLES

What do we mean when we talk about the tactical game model? We mean, as X. Tamarit says, a group of behaviours that we want our players to learn and that they manifest regularly and systematically within the four game phases - attack, defence, the transition

from attack to defence and the transition from defence to attack. It should consist of a series of major principles and their sub-principles within each phase and moment of the game.

These major principles will be the general behaviours that the coaches want our team to master, both individually and collectively. The sub-principles are more specific behaviours within those general behaviours. Therefore it is very important that they are interrelated, interconnected, follow a thread and are consistent. For example, an attacking principle would be the circulation of the ball from the initiation zone in defence with one of it's sub-principles being the width of the defensive line. We can analyse what is coherent - we cannot circulate the ball correctly and effectively out of defence if our players are all too close together.

We can apply the "Expansive Football" game model when we have an appropriate context and players with the correct profile. Although we firmly believe that as human beings we are intelligent and can adapt and evolve, anything can be learnt. If you firmly believe in an idea, have faith in it and work hard, it can be achieved. We believe in work, because that means training.

We outline the major principles and some sub-principles of the four phases that make up the game model for a team that wants to play "Expansive Football" in the tables/diagrams on the following pages. Each coach will add and apply his own principles, using his experience and knowledge of the players in his team, adding his own sub-principles (the specific behaviours he wants his team to perform).

GAME PHASES

We mentioned before that the game and the players are one and the same so consequently the game phases, attack and defence, cannot be separated. One phase conditions the other, you attack as you defend. We are in

all of the phases, all of the time. When we are submerged in one phase, how we act conditions all of the other phases as we are also thinking about them and that is why we say that we can find a little bit of each phase in any part of the game in. Phases are not figuratively represented as compact, separate and well defined blocks. When we are on the attack we are in a transition into defence in order to defend, and we are doing all of this all at the same time. We must prioritise one phase over another and some behaviours over others. Whilst we are within one phase, we are also within the others.

Gerard Pinies told us that, *"When we are defending we have to think about those movements that, at the same time, will allow us to attack. In the same way, when we attack we should have the security of defending at the same time".*

The instant that a player makes a move in attack we must be secure in the knowledge that he is protected by the teammates closest to him as well as those furthest away, helping the player through movement and being available in support.

As Lillo affirms, *"The game is an indivisible unit, there are no attacking movements without defensive movements. Both constitute a functional unit".* And Mourinho, *"I do not dissociate where the organisation begins whether in defence or attack. I do not analyse things so analytically."*

Therefore we should place the major principles and the principles of the other phases in this chapter, even though the book is dedicated to the attacking phase.

1. Attacking Phase

2. Transition from Attack to Defence

3. Defensive Phase

4. Transition from Defence to Attack

Attacking Phase

PRINCIPLES OF THE 4 GAME PHASES

1. ATTACKING PHASE	2. TRANSITION FROM ATTACK TO DEFENCE
Major Principle: *"Circulate the ball quickly, making the pitch bigger".* This is a major principle which makes the difference between our team and many others because we are talking about spatial organisation (big pitch) and time (quick movement). To accomplish this, remember that we must have a good positional game and balance.	**Major Principle:** Press the player with the ball and build the compact defensive block to be organised with good positioning in defence.
Principles: 1. Width, depth and diagonal play in attack. 2. Continuous support for the player on the ball to provide continuity. 3. Start play on one side and finish on the other to begin to progress deeper. 4. Maximum of 4 passes in one zone, then move to another. 5. Play outside to be able to play inside. 6. Dribble to draw, attract and divide. 7. Look for the third man, either near or far. 8. Create numerical superiority (at least a 2v1 both on the wing and inside). 9. Continuous movement and interchanging of positions. 10. If you move up and can progress, do not play backwards. 11. Optimal distance relationships. 12. Be aware of the players furthest away.	**Principles:** 1. Immediate and aggressive pressuring of the player with the ball. 2. Close passing lines to possible and probable recipients. 3. Recover the ball close to the opposition's goal. 4. Close lines, rebuild the defensive unit. 5. Reduce space in all directions; width, depth and diagonally. 6. Link up to provide cover, double marking, changing positions. 7. Make the most of the opposition's defensive disorganisation to win the ball back or reorganise defensively. 8. Distinguish whether the ball is "covered" or "uncovered". 9. "Elastic defence" to play the opponents offside. 10. Optimal distance relationships. 11. Be aware of the players furthest away.
Table: 'Principles of the 4 Game Phases'	

3. DEFENSIVE PHASE	4. TRANSITION FROM DEFENCE TO ATTACK
Major Principle: As a compact team, create an effective defensive situation against the player with the ball and possible and probable recipients, near and far.	**Major Principle:** Get the ball from the recovery zone.
Principles: 1. Keep a high defensive line to apply pressure. 2. Close the defensive line from outside to inside, wide and deep, maintaining a compact defensive block (especially in the middle of the pitch). 3. Push the opponent to an area where we can best apply pressure. 4. Continual movement; covering, interchanging of positions and double marking. 5. Create numerical superiority in the active zone (defensive density). 6. Track back or move up depending on whether the ball is covered" or uncovered. 7. "Elastic defence" to play the opponents offside. 8. Optimal distance relationships. 9. Be aware of the players furthest away.	**Principles:** 1. Get the ball out of the recovery zone to a nearby player in a good position who will be the person who decides on the type of attack. 2. Discriminate between depth (quick counter attack) or keeping possession (combined attack). 3. Open up, attack wide, deep and diagonally. 4. Look for areas where we have numerical and spacial superiority to play "Expansive Football". 5. Optimal distance relationships. 6. Be aware of the players furthest away.
Table: 'Principles of the 4 Game Phases'	

Depending on the phase of the game we are in we will use some principles or others on the basis that they are all interrelated and interconnected. We press aggressively high up the pitch, retrieving the ball close to the opponent's goal because we want to play "Expansive Football" and play in the opposition half. If we were pegged back in our own half this would be much more difficult.

Each coach has his principles/sub-principles according to his game model and he has to take into account not only the players, but the context as well. Training is not the same in Spain as it is in Italy or Finland. Every player has his own football and social culture and the game model that made us winners with one team is not viable with another team in another country.

ADAPTING TO THE OPPOSITION

The game model will serve us for the whole season and should be a fundamental part of pre-season training as this is the time when we lay the foundations of our game.

Throughout the year we will work micro-cycle to micro-cycle (one week), that is, game to game. Each week we will apply the corresponding content of the game model and we will execute our operational strategy which is our plan of action based on what we know about our opponent's characteristics (Anton).

As M. Monteleone and M.A. Ortega Jiménez explains, *"The operational strategy influences the training content so that we can make maximum use of the opponent's weaknesses and minimise the threat of their strengths. This does not mean that we change our game model every game, it simply means that we should work on some of the principles of our model to make it more difficult for our opponents".*

For example, we have studied our opponents and come to the conclusion that their left wing is their weak area as they do not press the winger and wing back aggressively. Our goalkeeper would then always initiate an attacking move on our left so that the ball makes its way over to the right and we can move deeper down this channel and exploit the space. We keep applying "Expansive Football" to make good use of their weaknesses.

We repeat that it is important to understand, and make the players understand that we do not change our game model depending on the opponent because we cannot ask our players to change and become something that they are not. We ask them simply to prioritise certain behaviours over others. This is why the operational strategy should be referred to within the game model.

We do not need to highlight the importance of scouting in the operational strategy. We must scout both individuals and teams.

We should know the strengths and weaknesses of our opponents through every phase of the game, including dead ball situations, as well as which players are the most dangerous, what zones we should pay more attention to and if they have players that link up particularly well.

UNDERSTANDING THE STRENGTHS AND WEAKNESSES OF THE OPPOSITION

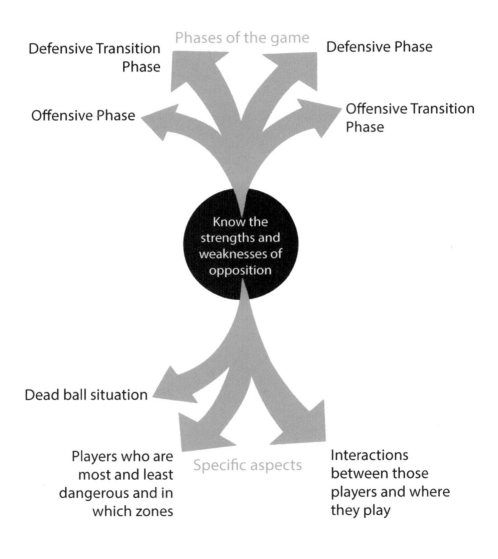

Phases of the game

Defensive Transition Phase

Defensive Phase

Offensive Phase

Offensive Transition Phase

Know the strengths and weaknesses of opposition

Dead ball situation

Players who are most and least dangerous and in which zones

Specific aspects

Interactions between those players and where they play

MICRO CYCLE TEMPLATE

We apply our game model and our operational strategy throughout the micro-cycle. If we trained 5 days a week our work would be dived as so:

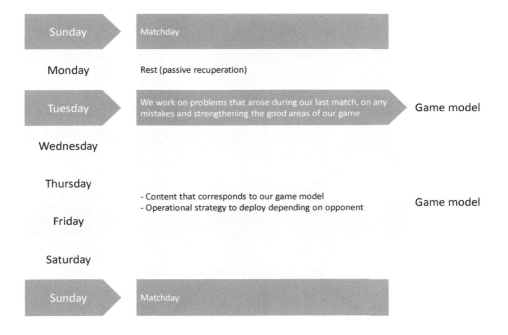

We see that we work on our tactical game model every day and it will be this way throughout the season, letting the players be themselves and guiding them towards being all that they can be.

FACTORS WITHIN OUR GAME MODEL

It is very important that the part of the game model that we work on and strengthen is directly related to the operational strategy so that there are no inconsistencies For the players. This useful diagram shows how to make a game model in which we combine all of these factors:

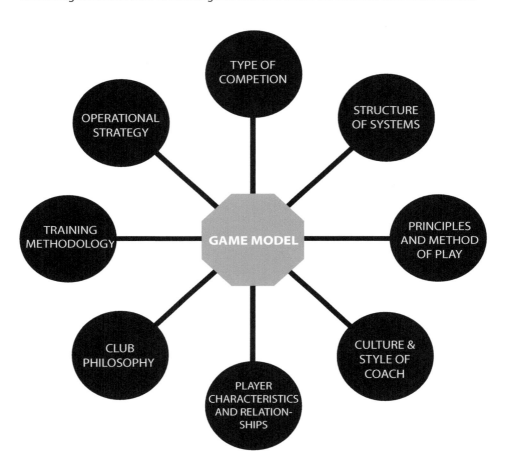

CHAPTER 7

Putting the Theory into Practice

PUTTING THE THEORY INTO PRACTICE

Now for the practical part. Theory is very important but putting it into practice is the most important thing of all.

In this chapter, we outline various "Expansive Football" situations dedicated to the movement of the ball from one side of the pitch to the other. This is not simply to move the actual ball but to move your opponents, to find and create space between them and to use it well.

A very important concept to remember is that it is not enough to have drills/practices that look good on paper. You must also know how to bring drills to life, to work and/or train them and prioritise structures for the players to learn - through the use of corrections, suitable information and constant feedback. Above all, the players need to understand the aim of the practice. Remember that through these practices we are working on our game model and our principles and their suitability for the players that we have - although everything is trainable. If you have a different context or another game model, perform different and more suitable drills/practices that fit your game model to efficiently and effectively reach your objectives. Each team is a micro-system within a macro-system, a world within a world. No two teams are the same and consequently have different needs and we as coaches must adapt to that.

If we follow the systemic methodologies we know that the physical aspect is just as relevant as the other spheres. However, in this chapter we focus mainly on the technical-tactical aspect. All of these drills/practices are tactical - positions, functions, roles etc. We will look at it from an "Expansive Football" perspective so we therefore need to optimise time. You don't have to train more, just better.

Each coach should set each training session for the specific day in the micro-cycle

(explanation to follow) and according to the circumstances. Not all teams train on the same days, some squads train 5 times a week, some 4, some 3 etc. The coach should use each session to focus on what he thinks the team need which is why we have not presented it daily, nor with physical parameters.

CREATING CONTEXTS FOR LEARNING

Remember that we have created certain contexts to promote certain behaviours. We unite this idea with an interesting concept from Chema Sanz: *"As coaches we should look to create certain contexts so that the players can see and learn what each others capabilities are. We must take into account the complexity of each element and the relationships established between them, determining that any modification of one of these will have an immediate repercussion on the others. The player will perform differently depending on the context in which he finds himself".*

It is important to understand that each session should be aimed at improving "Expansive Football" and that certain behaviours emerge. The player should be continually thinking, following the chain; perception (compiling information), mental solution (decision making) and a motor solution to the problem (physical-technical execution with tactical intent). This last concept, tactical intent, is what makes the difference. There is a study that reveals that an elevated percentage of passing errors are not a result of bad execution but of poor decision making and badly chosen solutions.

We should stimulate and develop the intelligence of the player and extend the four tactical concepts described by Lillo and J. Cuadrado Pino:

1. **TACTICAL CULTURE** (awareness of solutions to different situations)

2. **TACTICAL MEMORY** (remembering these solutions)

3. **TACTICAL INTELLIGENCE** (choosing the best solution for each situation)

4. **TACTICAL ABILITY** (knowing how to apply the solution)

To do this we must create common, important contexts, creating intelligent players that understand the game and know how to look for the same appropriate solutions to each problem. We must use drills/practices in which the player must continually apply himself mentally.

SUPPORTING AND PROTECTING THE PLAYERS

We must be proactive and resilient in order to play this type of positional attack. This is achieved through a lot of good work in training. We believe that doubts enter our heads when we lose the ball while playing it out of defence. We as coaches have to be able to make the players understand that it does not matter if we lose the ball, what is important is that we solve the problem. We should have thought about and trained every single thing that can happen in a game so that when it happens we know how to solve it.

Football is a game in which we train not only to improve but also to reduce the unknown through predicting behaviour. When a player misplaces a pass and doubts enter his head he is more likely to launch a long ball. Above everything, we should train the players to be confident and resilient, able to fight frustration, learn from their mistakes and

apply the solutions that they have worked on and learnt.

The player should feel protected. As Arjol says, the group thinks according to how they feel and then perform accordingly. If the team feels protected they will feel able to try things and act as a large group. When Guardiola made his debut as Barcelona coach in the league opener they lost against Numancia. This defeat did not change his style and his players, seeing that nothing changed day to day, began to grow in confidence and eventually exploded. *"One is not defeated by being beaten by an opponent but when you resign yourself to defeat".*

TWO FUNDAMENTAL DRILL FACTORS

Finally, when we have structured these drills/practices we have taken two fundamental factors into account:

1. A cognitive component

2. Concepts of the game must be interrelated as one cannot be separated from the other.

One conditions the other in a continuous sequence of concepts and phases; attack, transitions, defence, transitions.

When we say that they must have a cognitive component we mean that the player should always be thinking and be conditioned to be able to solve any situational problem that he is faced with. They should be similar contexts to those that they will find on match day. In summary, they are situational practices meaning drills with situations to resolve that which closely resemble real game problems.

PLAYER UNDERSTANDING OF TRAINING PURPOSE

The players should be aware of the importance of training and should train not only to play but to be the best. The performances will improve, more on a group than an individual level. Winning is not the most important thing, although obviously it is what makes us want to continue to coach. We must always be thinking. Playing badly and winning is "bread for today and hunger for tomorrow". Playing well is very important because it is what brings you closer to victory. The work of a coach is a labour of love that brings rewards in the long term. As Manuel Conde says: *"After extraordinary efforts there are extraordinary rewards".*

Paco Seirul.lo said that it is important that the player understands the nature of each drill/practice and what he should be expected to learn from it before having it explained to him. The player should know what the coach is trying to get from him with any given situation, requiring him to concentrate and pay more attention, thus learn more.

THE SANDWICH METHOD

We want to highlight a very useful psychology technique used to correct mistakes called the "Sandwich Method". This, as Jose Maria Buceta explains, is a technique used to correct a mistake (the cheese in the sandwich) in between two positive comments (the bread). The first comment is about something that the player has done well, the second addresses the mistake and the third should reinforce the praise for the correct action. The organisation of the "sandwich" in relation to "Expansive Football" is as follows:

- Recognition of a positive action performed by the player e.g. "Very good support play, excellent".

- Correction of the mistake (explanation and demonstration by the coach and correct performance of the behaviour by the player) e.g. "Position your body better to get a better view of the pitch".

- Social reinforcement of the correct behaviour e.g. "Very good", "that's it" and applause or positive gestures.

WORKING EXAMPLE TO PUT THIS INTO PRACTICE

As we have commented before, it is very important that the coach does not only create drills/practices on paper, but puts them into practice. He must know how to get them across to his team, motivating his players and making them believe in what they are doing. Eventually the work will pay off.

In the table on the following page we demonstrate the union between the contents of the training and the game model in this micro-cycle. Our operational strategy within the game model is formed by addressing what happened in the last game and what we know about our next opponents. We have chosen difficult opponents against which we will apply "Expansive Football". This basic table highlights the most important aspects in very general terms.

OPERATIONAL STRATEGY WITHIN OUR GAME MODEL

Day: ____	Session No: ____	Micro-cycle: _____

Content of the Game Model That We Will Strengthen in this Micro-Cycle	In this Micro-Cycle we will strengthen the attacking phase of "Expansive Football". **Principle:** "Keep/maintain possession of the ball" **Sub-principles:** 1. "Play safe passes" - take no risks, make a safe pass to the teammate in the optimal position to ensure that we maintain possession. 2. Start again - if we cannot progress we look backwards to start again and look for new channels of progression. 3. Vary the spaces we use to progress so that we are not predictable. 4. Progressive interactive criteria: 1. Keep the ball individually. 2. Keep the ball by playing triangles. 3. Keep the ball collectively. 5. ...
Previous Opponents ,...............................,	We observed: • We did not circulate the ball well in attack and did not play fluid "Expansive Football". • We were aggressive and quick in recovering the ball during defensive transitions (transition from attack to defence). • We were tight and together defensively and did not give away any goals. • During the transition from defence to attack we played the ball out of the recovery zone correctly, playing "Expansive Football".

Next Opponents	**Team from the bottom half of the table, who play 4-4-2**
....	• **Attack:** They use a direct attack, always leaving 2 strikers forward who play off the back of the opposition's defence. They do not score many rebounds as the forwards play and move quickly and far away from the midfielders who stay back and separate. • **Transition from Defence to Attack:** The player that has lost the ball applies pressure and his teammates track back quickly to zone 1 or 2. • **Defence:** They use an accumulative defence with 9 players (including the goalkeeper) behind the ball. They do not give away many goals. They defend wide and have fixed points of pressure on the flanks leaving a lot of space in the central area. • **Transition from Attack to Defence:** They counter attack very quickly when they recover the ball and attack vertically through the 2 strikers. They are at their most dangerous during this phase. • **Dead ball situations:** ... • **Individual Players and/or Dangers:** ... • **Relationships and/or Certain Players Strengths:** ...
Conclusion of the Micro-Cycle Week	This week we will work mainly on the transition phases (attack to defence and defence to attack): • The circulation of the ball, "Expansive Football" to disorganise the opposition defence and allow us to penetrate, particularly out wide • We will continue to strengthen defensive transitions to avoid being attacked on the counter. Specific operational strategy: • The left centre back does not correctly cover his wing back, is not close enough to him and leaves too much space between them. We can make the most of these spaces by playing a 2v1 against the opposition's wing back using our winger and wing back or winger and centre midfielder, playing one-twos and then losing our markers and breaking to penetrate these zones.

Tactical Phases Sessions	**ATTACKING PHASE** **Major Principle:** Circulate the ball quickly, making the pitch bigger. **Principles:** 1. Width, depth and diagonal play in attack. 2. Continuous support for the player with the ball to provide continuity. 3. Start on one side and finish on the other to then progress deeper. 4. Play on the outside to be able to play on the inside. **Sub-Principles:** 1. Continuous involvement of the full backs on the opposite wing (passive zones) to provide width, depth and diagonal angles. 2. Each player that receives the ball should have 4 solutions close by; one on the right, one on the left, one in front and one behind, creating a rhombus with the player in possession inside and always within an optimum distance. 3. When the ball arrives on the opposite wing look for a 2v1 with the last pass being the assist through to the breaking strikers or inside players 4. When a player receives the ball out wide his teammates should make sure that they are staggered with the midfielders, strikers and defensive midfielder all providing different solutions
	TRANSITION FROM ATTACK TO DEFENCE **Major Principle:** Pressure the player with the ball and rebuild the compact defensive block to maintain an organised positional defence. **Principles:** 1. Apply pressure immediately and aggressively to the player with the ball. 2. Mark the players who are furthest away and the most dangerous. 3. Recover the ball close to the opposition goal. **Sub-Principles:** 1. A player applying pressure to the player with the ball should position his body in a way that blocks a long pass to the forwards. 2. Defenders closely mark the players likely to be involved in a counter attack, while there is always a free player in defence plus the goalkeeper who moves slightly away from his goal line. 3. Press very high mainly against the strikers and midfielders with a minimum of 2 players aggressively pressuring the player with the ball, because if he manages to play a long ball into space for his striker to run on to we might be vulnerable.

OTHER OBJECTIVES TO PRIORITISE

Socio-Affective:

Defensive and attacking cooperation to reach the team's objectives.

The Power of Will and Self Confidence:

Build players' self-confidence after they have learned and trained how you want them to play, both in defence and attack.

Develop will, determination and perseverance in achieving objectives. Adapt to uncertain situations and strive for continuous improvement in quality, and competitive spirit.

Socio-Affective:

Promote other efficient solutions to any uncertain situation (Arjol).

Observation Example:

We are playing away on a pitch measuring......... This is very long and wide, perfect for playing "Expansive Football", for finding free space but is also good for our opponents to counter attack.

EXPANSIVE FOOTBALL TRAINING SESSION

What follows is a typical "Expansive Football" session, based on what we have previously highlighted. The operational strategy and the principles of the game model that we will work on are included in two parts (training 5 days a week). Two days are dedicated to the development phase and the other two days are dedicated to the consolidation phase, remembering that we always dedicate the first day of the micro-cycle to correcting mistakes from the previous game and promoting the successes that form part of the correction phase.

DEVELOPMENT PHASE

This "Expansive Football" session is for a day in the development phase. On the other day we will work on the transition from attack to defence. The order is secondary, as one can be a Wednesday and the other a Thursday or the other way around. We will work on all of the phases in each session, but what we work on will depend on our operational strategy, game model and behaviours.

CONSOLIDATION PHASE

The other two days are used to focus on the consolidation phase. On the penultimate day we work on these two phases and the principles of them equally. While in the last session we practice dead ball situations and go over the specifics of what we have worked on throughout the week as well as any other aspects of the specific operational strategy that we may encounter during the game.

It is important to remember that in every session dedicated to the consolidation phase you must also influence the phase chosen in the operational strategy with its specific principles, but the other phases should also be worked on.

For example, in the "Expansive football" session that we outline, we work on and strengthen our attacking phase as well as the transitional phase from attack to defence. For example the "immediate and aggressive pressuring of the player on the ball" principle, using the rule of provocation (or "rules of specific tactical behaviours" that we will explain in later chapters) and applying this to each drill - when you lose the ball you must retrieve it immediately because whoever stole it can shoot directly at goal, without opposition. This rule states that whoever loses the ball and the players closest to him immediately apply pressure to retrieve it as the player who stole the ball can shoot at goal without the goalkeeper's intervention. This simulates one of the next opponent's strengths - retrieving the ball and linking up quickly with their forwards.

Remember that we must look to enhance the content of the sessions, principles and game model. We use a suitable operational strategy so that there is consistency in training, enabling the development and a transfer of knowledge of each principle to the players. This way the players know exactly what the coach wants this week and throughout the year. In this way, the players perfectly learn the game model without any confusion.

THE TRAINING WEEK

Sunday	Matchday

Monday	Rest (passive recuperation)

Tuesday	We work on problems that arose during our last match, on any mistakes and strengthening the good areas of our game	Game model

Wednesday

Thursday

- Content that corresponds to our game model
- Operational strategy to deploy depending on opponent   Game model

Friday

Saturday

Sunday	Matchday

| DAY: ___ | SESSION NO: ___ | MICRO-CYCLE: _____ |
| | | MESO-CYCLE: _____ |

| *Strengthening the Game Model* | **Principle "ATTACKING PHASE":**

"Keep/maintain possession of the ball".

Sub-Principles:

1. "Play safe passes" - take no risks, make a safe pass to the teammate in the optimal position to ensure that we maintain possession.

2. Start again - if we cannot progress we look backwards to start again and look for new channels of progression.

3. Vary the spaces we use to progress so that we are not predictable.

4. Progressive interactive criteria: a) Keep the ball individually, b) Keep the ball by playing triangles, c) Keep the ball collectively. |
| *ATTACKING PHASE (Priority Phase)*

Type of attack: Positional "Expansive Football" | **Major Principle:**

Circulate the ball quickly making the pitch bigger.

Principles:

1. Width, depth and diagonal play in attack.

2. Continuous support for the player with the ball to provide continuity.

3. Start on one side and finish on the other to then progress deeper.

4. Play on the outside to be able to play on the inside.

Sub-Principles:

1. Continuous involvement of the wing backs on the opposite wing (passive zones) to provide width, depth and diagonal angles.

2. Each player that receives the ball should have 4 solutions close by; one on the right, the left, in front and behind, creating a rhombus with the player in possession, always within an optimum distance.

3. When the ball arrives on the opposite wing look for a 2v1 with the last pass being the assist through to the breaking strikers or inside players.

4. When a player receives the ball out wide his teammates should make sure that they are staggered with the midfielders, strikers and defensive midfielder all providing different solutions. |

SECONDARY PHASE:	**Major Principle:**
	Pressure the player with the ball.
Transition from Defence to Attack	**Principle:**
	Immediate and aggressive pressuring of the player with the ball.
	Sub-Principle:
	The player who goes to apply pressure to the player with the ball should position his body in a way that blocks a long pass to the forwards.

CHAPTER 8

METHODS OF TRAINING

METHODS OF TRAINING

THE CONSCIOUS AND UNCONSCIOUS MIND

It has been scientifically demonstrated that the human brain only uses about 15% of it's potential. We also know that it learns through ideas, concepts and images, not just through information but through everything that we do and through the experiences that we are living through. Consequently, training and drills are the base from which we learn.

To save time and energy the human brain passes what it learns in the conscious to the subconscious. The conscious part selects the useful behaviours and derives them from the subconscious. Make sure that what is stored are not unwanted behaviours as they will automate the subconscious.

CREATING POSITIVE LEARNING EXPERIENCES

Experience is vital. It is not enough to simply say it but we must work on it so the human being perceives it and lives it and has as many positive experiences as possible. Emotions help people to learn, therefore the coach must know how to develop drills that produce positive emotions in the players. They must be drills that they enjoy, producing positive sensations and satisfaction. The pleasure strengthens and improves learning. Antonio Damasio (quoted by X. Tamarit) said that *"People, both consciously and subconsciously seek things that cause pleasure and run from things that cause pain and sadness. When these positive emotions are associated with specific actions/activities, they tend to be performed more frequently and with more conviction".* What do footballers like the most?

To play. Paradoxically, what we must do is look for training drills in which our players play football so that we can substitute the word "train" for "play". We must use situations that deliver a high level of learning that can bring the players pleasure and, because we repeat it, the player loves playing. The drills/practices that we develop should predominantly include tactics. The player should think and play, experiencing the game.

ANTICIPATION

Everything that we learn is used to increase speed. If the brain is faced with a situation that it recognises it acts quickly but still must think and search for stored information. It will take a lot of time if it has to take into account and work through all of the variables. Through training we should prepare the player to anticipate the answers when faced with real game situations. This is where the phrase "play as you train" comes from. Previously this has referred to aspects of physical intensity etcetera, but this is no longer the case. It also means focusing on situations that could occur in a real game. We do not say that we train but that we play, and on match day we do the same thing - play.

As Adrian Cervera said, *"The regular performance of the principle actions of the game model created for our team makes the players believe they have a familiarity with a functioning logic that allows us to anticipate with more efficiency and less effort the events happening within a game".* The concept of anticipation is fundamental in football as well as in life. The player anticipates what can happen, recognising the situation and using the most appropriate solution that he knows. The human brain makes a copy of what it has

experienced so that when it happens again it knows quickly how to act. The player should understand the situation in order to store the correct solution so must live it, experience it and above all understand it. This is why it is important that the players understand what you are looking for in the drills - what you are looking for and why.

EMOTIONAL TRIGGERS

Somatic markers (mechanisms by which emotional processes can guide behaviour and particularly decision making) are vital to learning. According to an online article in "Football Dominante", that defines them as "the signal from the stimuli that allows us to have more efficient decision making and reasoning processes". In essence it is a 'flag' that causes a response in our body.

The somatic markers hugely influence decision making at any given moment, producing a subjective emotional reaction. The emotions influence the decision making and the decision making influences our emotions and our perception, creating a database of life experiences that help to develop and enhance a somatic marker. Like traffic lights, when we see a red light, our body stops. If we see a green light it lets us go. The somatic markers send signals to our body from the database of our life, recording the situations and experiences.

CORRECT DECISION MAKING

Consequently, well organised and structured training will consolidate the correct decision making processes within the player's 'database'. Creating rigid automatic responses reduces the players instinctive answers and discourages him from thinking.

The time it takes to make a decision and the quality of the solution are what makes the

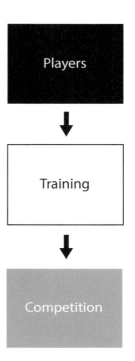

difference. Contextualised and structured training is essential for the players to reach high levels of decision making, thus providing the appropriate responses in match situations.

PREPARING FOR MATCH DAYS

With the exercises or methods that we will present in this chapter (all references in applying "Expansive Football") the footballer will acquire certain behaviours that are solutions to certain situations that he will encounter on match days. We train so that the team knows what to expect on match days. In fact, the primary objective of each coach is to take the training and impart it on the players that he directs while at the same time predicting what will happen on match days.

Following this approach, we see that the players, the training and the competition should all be related and resemble each other:

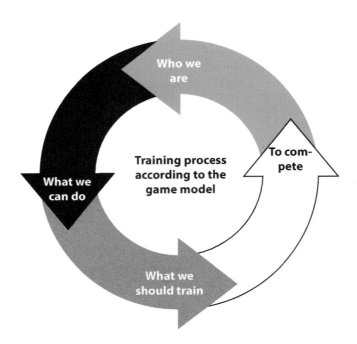

IT IS ABOUT THE PLAYERS

Training should enhance what the players are and what they can become. It is not what we want them to feel obligated to do according to our ideas, but what we want them to do which is directly related to what they can and know how to do. Training is meant to improve/help develop these skills, qualities and the potential that the player has. This should not be done in an isolated and detached way but collectively with his teammates.

For this to happen it is vital that the players understand this themselves and are conscious of it and from there the coaches should create common context. We must create situations in training where the players recognise the behaviours that we want them to repeat and continue to manifest, following the team's game model. We must identify who we are, predicting what we can do and above all, what we should train in order to be prepared for competition.

INDIVIDUAL AND COLLECTIVE SOLUTIONS

Being prepared for match day means that when they find themselves in a situation, the players can interpret it and search their memory for an appropriate solution that has been worked on in training. As "Football Concept" states *"Footballers can provide a solution to all of the contexts within a game and by extension all members of the team perform the same interpretation to act in a coordinated manner, in harmony, together...".*

This does not mean that they think and act the same when faced with the same situation. That is impossible and we cannot ask for that because each player is unique and has his own way of thinking. He will never act in the same way even when faced with an identical situation because he and the context will have changed. There are coaches who believe that the whole team should think the same when faced with a problem, but we do not.

The team is a living organism the same as a human being. Humans are made up of different systems i.e. Respiratory, digestive etc. We have vital organs and when faced with the same problem they all interact, looking for a common solution but they act differently according to their natures. For example, the heart pumps blood around the body faster, the lungs dilate more to let more oxygen in. Together, the systems that make up the human body perform their functions to create a solution to the problem. They work together but act differently, because each organ has it's own mission and specific function. Without one it would be difficult for the others to function. They are connected and interpret the problem the same but react differently.

The same thing happens in football. Each player has his mission and his way of dealing with a problem but the footballer should relate the solution to what is happening within the team. In "Expansive Football" when faced with a situation where one midfielder moves closer to the other midfielder to receive a pass and is able to turn, the full back will, at the same time, push up the wing as he knows that when the ball crosses the pitch the winger will receive it in space deep on the flank. Faced with the same situation one player moves closer and the other moves further away. They act differently but are interconnected!

The footballer should create his own solutions when faced with circumstances that can change from moment to moment, but his solutions should always be from the point of view of the team, their nature and the game model that we have applied. To repeat, it is the interactions and relationships between the players that counts.

REINFORCING THE GAME MODEL THROUGH DRILLS

It is important to generate contexts so that the player strengthens his capabilities in

relation to the team's game plan. So, it is vital that each drill/practice not only has a physical objective and uses a ball, but is also specific to our game model. This way the player is constantly working, learning and reinforcing what he has learnt, always in relation to how our team wants to play, both individually and collectively.

The drill should have logical and coherent transference of real game situations. If we want to play a positional attack, what good is it if in training we only practice drills where the players trap the ball? It does not make sense. Conversely, if we want to play a direct attacking game we would not train with small possession games in tight spaces.

The game model should govern the training and guide the entire process. Depending on where we are within the training session, whether in the warm up, training or cool down, we can use situational drills that contain the following three characteristics:

1. **COOPERATIVE** (teammates, socio-affective)

2. **COMPETITIVE** (opposition, feeling of togetherness, emotional will/desire to win)

3. **COGNITIVE** (tactical intelligence)

We have divided the methods into 4 categories:

1. **ANALYTICAL**

2. **IPTE** (Interrelated physical-technical methods)

3. **IPTETA** (Interrelated physical-technical-tactical methods)

4. **POSITIONAL GAMES**

THE 4 TRAINING METHODS WITHIN OUR GAME MODEL

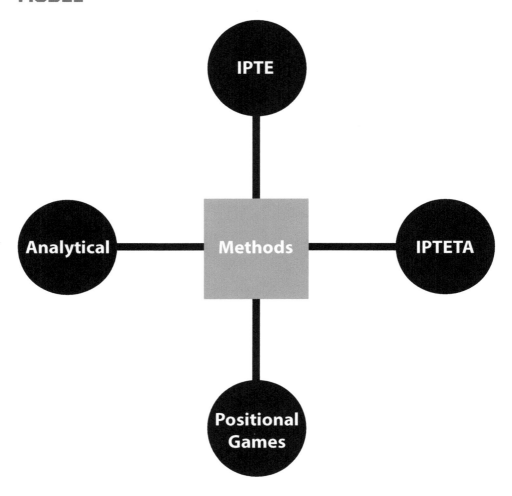

ANALYTICAL METHODS

Analytical methods are drills/practices in which there is no football apart from the logic of the game itself. We can use a ball without it being related to football. We have divided them into two groups:

1. Methods without the ball (continuous running, power circuits without the ball etc.)

2. Methods with the ball (start up games with a ball such as a game of football using the hands, handball etc.)

These drills/practices can be useful as everything is useful in football if there is a reason for it. There is nothing specific in these exercises and they are not within our game model so we will not expand on them in this book.

IPTE METHODS

Interrelated Physical-Technical (IPTE) methods consist of a motor exercise with motor execution and technical execution because gestural technical actions appear. They are interrelated because they need each other and one influences the other.

The methods in this category are mostly 'targeted', composed of technical wheels or shapes with "pass and move" characteristics, to the space previously occupied by the player that passed you the ball. It works better as part of the warm up or at the start of the main training session, so you can add joint or ball movements and vary the intensity.

The majority of these methods are designed around a 4-3-3 formation but they should all maintain the essence and identity of our tactical game model. They do not feature tactical intelligence as such, in that the player must think and make decisions, although they should always be specifically directed towards our game model. They are cooperative (passes between teammates), but they are not competitive (there is no opposition), nor cognitive (the player should not have to think tactically to resolve the situation).

The following exercises involve continual repetition of the desired action. They are closed, lineal, contextual drills for which the players already know the answers.

These drills should follow three rules, as Jose Luis Arjol tells us:

1. They should never stop. If a ball is wayward, the player takes another ball or if one player makes a mistake his teammates fix it.

2. Any problem that crops up during the game is solved by the players playing it.

3. Players must be able to respond on the run to the coach's instructions, e.g. A change of direction, number of touches etc.

We have divided the methods in this section into five sub-sections:

1. **"Technical wheels or technical patterns"** (e.g. a technical pattern drill applied to our formation)

2. **Physical circuit interrelated with technical** (e.g. an explosive strength circuit with one strength exercise followed by a technical exercise)

3. **Automation without opposition** (interlinked with coordination, e.g. Performing a coordination drill before and evolution drill)

4. **Technical-tactical actions within the game model** (technical actions within some specific movements established in our game model)

5. **Awareness and body positioning with a ball** (movements with some type of technical action before or after it and should always be related to our game model)

The IPTE methods can be applied to a:

- **Group** (a small number of players)

- **Sector** (any single line - defence, midfield or attack)

- **Inter-sectoral** (two or more interlinked lines)

You can use opposition although they should be passive.

In many IPTE drills, especially those used as a warm up, you can begin with a ball and perform articular mobility or movements and then introduce more balls and increase the rhythm.

IPTETA METHODS

Interrelated Physical-Technical-Tactical (IPTETA) methods are drills in which tactics are a protagonist, meaning that the player needs to think to resolve uncertain random situations. We see tactical intelligence alongside physical movement and technical actions. The players must know how to adapt to an open context and solve it through learning the specific behaviours that we want them to use on match days.

They are "specific and competitive" drills. They are open situations and they reflect the game that we want our players to play. They follow the principles of our team's tactical game model. There is cooperation (there are teammates), they are competitive (there are opponents), and they are cognitive (the player must think to resolve problems that appear in a game). This is why they are tactical.

There is a sequence of principles of the four phases:

1. ATTACKING PHASE

2. TRANSITION FROM ATTACK TO DEFENCE

3. DEFENSIVE PHASE

4. TRANSITION FROM DEFENCE TO ATTACK

As we have mentioned before, football and the moments within the game cannot be separated, as one conditions the other. When we are attacking we should think about defending and vice versa. The player should learn through these drills/practices what to do at any given time during the game. If we make our way up the pitch and end up taking a shot on goal the player should have learnt how to answer these questions:

a. What do I do if we don't score?

b. What do I do if the opposition steal the ball?

c. What will our defensive transition be?

Training this, we come to the "What happens if we get the ball back?" - Transition phase to counter attack, utilising depth and width. If we do not get the ball back we have a transition from attack to defence with pressing so that we can enter the defensive phase with movement, covering and a numerical superiority in and around the ball zone.

It is important that with these IPTETAs, the player knows which of our tactical game model principles to apply at any given moment. All of the team should interpret the situation and search for a solution according to their tactical role/mission.

We have divided the IPTETAs into six sub-sections:

1. **Tactical Games:** Drills with tactical rules, such as dividing the pitch into 3 channels and only being able to score a goal when the ball has passed through each channel.

2. **Attack versus Defence:** E.g. 3 midfielders and 3 attackers must score against defence.

3. **Automation with Opposition:** Evolutions with a small number of opposition such as 3 centre backs.

4. **Technical-Physical Circuit with Opposition:** E.g. Play a 3v2 but first perform some explosive sprints or technical actions.

5. **Sector Specific Situations:** Specific work in lines - drills focused on specific situations we could face against an opponent's midfield or defensive line.

6. **Games Prioritising Other Spheres:** Drills that perform a specific role relevant to other spheres e.g. A game one team is winning 1-0 with five minutes to go - we work on the mental aspects such as soaking up pressure or dealing with a counter attack.

As with the IPTE method, the player organisation within the IPTETAs could be:

- **Group** (a small number of players)

- **Sector** (any single line - defence, midfield or attack)

- **Inter-sectoral** (two or more interlinked lines)

The opposition should always be combative. To apply our "Expansive Football" model we have introduced *'the rules of specific tactical behaviours'* (that we will shortly explain in more detail) so that the footballer adapts to playing in a way that supports the development of our type of positional attack. As we said before, you cannot separate attack from defence in the IPTETAs so we have consequently applied a rule to every phase of the game to enable "Expansive Football" following our game model.

"The rules of specific tactical behaviours" appear in the majority of the IPTETAs and they have been developed with a view to improving "Expansive Football".

The rules of specific tactical behaviours are:

1. **In Attack -** If a high pass is not an assist we call it offside.

2. **In Defence -** If we retrieve the ball in the opposition's half the goal counts double.

3. **In Defensive Transitions -** When we lose the ball we must win it back immediately because the player that stole it can have a free shot on goal without the goalkeeper's intervention.

4. **In Attacking Transitions -** When we steal the ball we can have a free shot on goal without the intervention of the goalkeeper.

These rules favour our "Expansive Football" attacking game and by extension the other phases of our game model with the following rules:

- In attack we prefer to play to feet so we prohibit high passes unless they would be an assist, i.e. When there is a clear goal scoring opportunity.

- In defence we press very high up the pitch and steal the ball close to the opposition's goal, opening ourselves up.

- For the transition from attack to defence, when we lose the ball we press immediately to recover it before the player who stole it tries to shoot on goal.

- For the transition from defence to attack after recovering the ball we play at speed (although not hastily). Taking a shot at goal simulates the exit from the zone the ball was retrieved, where in theory there is a high density of opposition and we are being pressed.

There are other rules of a more general character that also influence the game:

a. If the ball is cleared, the team with the ball lose possession.

b. No limit on the maximum number of touches a player can take, but if the player on the ball is touched on the shoulder by another player's hand his team lose possession. This rule supports the creativeness and expressiveness of the player because sometimes he will be in situations where he needs to take more touches, e.g. When a player receives the ball and is alone so must dribble to draw the marker away from his teammate or free himself from a marker.

POSITIONAL GAME METHODS

The positional games are possession based through tactical roles and there is a correlation with the formation used (in this case 4-3-3) and with the specific role of each individual player. As M. Viscidi says *"It means that the players do not casually run around the pitch but they move across the terrain according to their position and mission"*.

M. Viscidi continues *"We are permitted to train the player in possession according to his position and mission and the formation that we use during a match, as well as in passing lines, losing a marker, control and anything else that is referred to as technical-tactical. Positional games are very specific"*.

The table demonstrates the difference between classic possession games and positional games from M. Viscidi's book:

CLASSIC POSSESSION	POSITIONAL GAMES
a. Possession of the ball is a priority	a. The positions are the priority
b. The players play wherever they want on the pitch	b. The players are in set positions on the pitch
c. The players move and lose their markers wherever they like	c. The players move and lose their markers according to their specific positions
d. There is not always numerical superiority	d. Numerical superiority is obligatory using utility players
e. There is improvisation	e. There is strict order
f. There is no direction	f. Each team is playing in a specific direction
g. There is no relationship with the formation	g. Improves the group collectively and also, by it's context, the individual
h. Improves the players individually but it is not transferable to the game	
Table: 'Positional Game Methods'	

In classic possession, the objective is maintaining possession of the ball and reaching a maximum number of passes. In positional games the priority is order, where the players are positioned within our formation. This is the main difference between the two. In positional games you train the associations and synergies between the players on the pitch who interact with each other - the full back with the winger, the attacking midfielder with the striker etc. In the classic possession game the logical positions are not respected.

In positional games it is very important to include neutral players to create a numerical superiority in attack. The positioning in the practices should be in accordance with their position in the team's formation. The defenders can be facing the attack or in their positions.

You can work on width (by placing the utility players out wide), on depth (by positioning the neutral players high up the pitch), on diagonal play or on all three of these.

You can work on diagonal play for example, with a reference player (striker) to receive the ball, by conquering a specific space on the pitch or by heading towards goal.

You can increase the number of players, starting with a 2v2 plus one neutral player until you have 9v9 plus two neutral players.

We have two types of positional game methods:

1. **Positional Games:** With a large number of players and a large space (inter-sectoral organisation)

2. **Positional Possession Games:** A reduced number of players with fixed positions (type of sectoral positional possession game)

SUMMARY OF THE METHODS OF TRAINING

To summarise this chapter, we have a useful table showing each of the four methods and their sub-sections, which are the drills/practices that we use to work on the attacking phase of "Expansive Football" and the other phases in our game model:

Remember that we do not want to limit the player's creativity which is why we allow free touches in all of the practices. The players should stay within the areas marked out by cones, especially the utility players as we want our players to play within a limited area. The utility players can take the ball out of the marked area by performing defensive actions such as interceptions, tackles etc.

The physical aspect will vary according to what each coach is looking for, the day of the micro-cycle and in which part of the training the drill is performed in. An IPTE technical possession game within the warm up on a Monday after match day will not be the same as an IPTE drill performed within the main training session on a Wednesday.

Each coach can vary these exercises as he sees fit and adapt them to his own tactical game model and formation etc.

1. ANALYTICAL	2. IPTE	3. IPTETA	4. POSITIONAL GAMES
i. Without the ball (running, physical circuits etc.) ii. With the ball (activation games, football tennis etc.)	i. Technical wheels or technical patterns ii. Physical circuits interlinked with technical iii. Automations without aggressive opposition iv. Technical-tactical actions within the game model v. Awareness and body shape with the ball	i. Tactical games ii. Attack vs defence iii. Automations with aggressive opposition iv. Technical-physical circuit with opposition v. Sector specific situations (work in lines) vi. Games prioritising other spheres	i. Positional games ii. Positional possession games
Table: 'Summary of the Methods of Training'			

CHAPTER 9

TRAINING PRACTICES

Warm Ups

Continuous Dribbling/Passing Warm Up

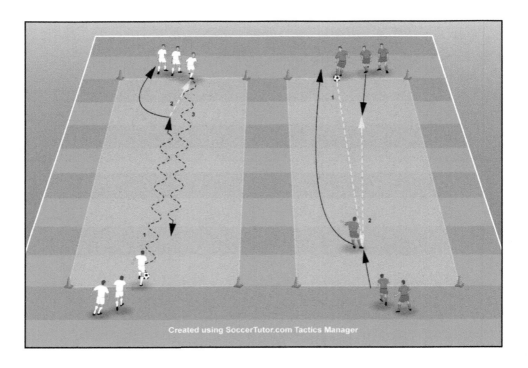

Created using SoccerTutor.com Tactics Manager

Objective

To be used as a warm up which incorporates game elements such as dribbling, player movement and passing.

Description

GROUP 1: The first player dribbles the ball forwards and then passes to the player opposite, before joining the queue at the end. The next player then does the same in the opposite direction. The sequence is continuous.

GROUP 2: The first player passes the ball to his teammate opposite and then runs to the other end. The second player moves forward to receive, passes to the next player in line and then runs to the other end. The sequence is continuous.

Coaching Point

Increase the speed of this exercise so the players start to work harder and nobody is standing still.

Positional 4 v 1 / 4 v 2 Possession Game

Created using SoccerTutor.com Tactics Manager

Objective

The attacking tactical objective is to create passing lines/angles and maintain possession. The defensive objective is to recover the ball and pass it quickly to the player next to him.

Description

In an 8 x 12 yard area, we can either play 4v1 or 4v2. The players are not in absolute set positions but position themselves in triangles and rhombus shapes.

When one of the middle players wins/intercepts the ball, they then play as if starting a counter attack. The player who lost the ball closes down the new ball carrier so they must demonstrate good decision making to quickly move the ball to start an attack e.g. If No.4 loses the ball, the middle player should quickly play the ball out wide to No.6 or No.3. If the pass to the outside is successful, the player who loses the ball swaps roles with the player who wins it and we continue.

Coaching Point

The players should be in the same positions that they would be in during a real game.

Technical Passing and Receiving in a Positional Practice

Created using SoccerTutor.com Tactics Manager

Objective

To practice receiving and passing in different positions on the pitch.

Description

We position two lines as shown in the diagram, attacking and defensive. The defensive line consists of five players (2 full backs, 2 centre backs and 1 defensive midfielder). The attacking line also consists of five players (2 wingers, 2 attacking midfielders and 1 striker).

The players start in their positions on the blue cones. We start with 2 balls simultaneously in the positions shown and play "pass and move" (to the next position). The passes are played in the sequence shown along both lines.

Coaching Points

1. We use this practice so that each player learns each teammate's role and how he should receive the pass and how he should pass the ball along the "chain". As Seirul.lo says, *"To understand the game you must play in all of the positions".*

2. If a pass is misplaced, quickly pass a new ball in.

3. To increase the speed and rhythm, introduce additional balls.

Tactical Small Sided Games

Building Up Play in a 6 Zone 9 v 9 Small Sided Game

Created using SoccerTutor.com Tactics Manager

Objective

To develop possession play with intelligent tactical movement and explosive physical movements (acceleration).

Description

Using half a full sized pitch, we play a 9v9 game. We divide the pitch into 6 zones as shown in the diagram. Each team has 8 outfield players and 1 goalkeeper.

One team starts with the ball and before they are allowed to try and score, the ball must be played through all 3 zones in the defensive half before being able to progress into the opposition's half, where again the team in possession have to play the ball through all 3 zones before attempting to score in the goal.

The players are not allowed to play from one corner to another within a square, but must instead play through the middle of the pitch. If the opposition win the ball, they must immediately pass the ball into another zone. At this point the game changes and we just have a normal game (attack vs defence).

Coaching Point

We must remember to include the full backs in an attack.

Attacking from Back to Front in an 8 v 6 Game with Cone Gates

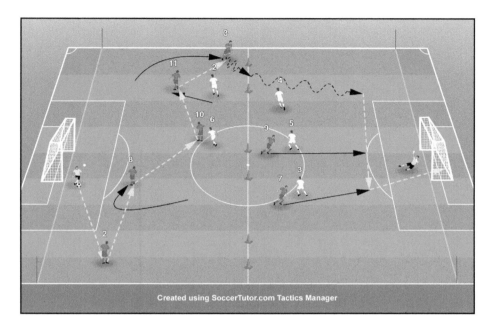

Created using SoccerTutor.com Tactics Manager

Description

Using a full pitch we have 7 red attacking players (2 full backs, 2 attacking midfielders, 2 wingers and 1 striker) against 5 white defending players (4 defenders and 1 defensive midfielder).

Before being allowed to try and score in the goal, the attacking team must first play the ball through one of the 3 cone gates positioned on the halfway line. They are not allowed to play directly from one winger to the other and must use the players in the centre.

The defenders move across to try and block them. If a defender wins the ball, they then have the same aim to play the ball through one of the 3 cone gates before trying to score at the opposite end.

Coaching Points

1. The attacking team should use the full backs to create 2v1 situations out wide.

2. The striker (9) stays in the opposition's half and acts as an outlet - we position him there to make the situation more real and to provide depth to the attack.

3. If the whites are attacking, their defensive midfielder (6) should be in line with the attacking team. The red striker stays in his position in line with the defence.

4. In the defensive phase the defensive midfielder should stay in line with the defence to provide cover etc.

Positional Play in a Dynamic 3 Team 5 v 5 (+4) Small Sided Game

Created using SoccerTutor.com Tactics Manager

Description

In the area shown, we have 3 teams of 4 players who all play in specific positions. The 2 teams inside have 1 defensive midfielder, 2 attacking midfielders and 1 striker. The team on the outside (2 wingers and 2 full backs) act as neutral players and play with the team in possession.

We play a normal 5v5 (+4) game but the ball must be passed to a neutral player before a goal can be scored. The first team to concede 2 goals moves to the outside and become neutral players. The utility players move inside and the game continues.

One neutral player cannot pass directly to another neutral player. If a team scores directly from a cross by a neutral player, the goal counts double. Any player who wins the ball can score directly without passing to a neutral player (this stimulates pressing to retrieve the ball).

Coaching Points

1. Limit the outside neutral players to 1 touch to speed up play.

2. Change the player positions often so they all learn different roles.

Physical and Technical Practices (IPTE)

Technical Passing Diamond with One-Two Combination

Created using SoccerTutor.com Tactics Manager

Objective

This is a technical passing practice with the tactical concept of using width and depth and tactical actions such as one-two combinations.

Description

In a 20 x 20 yard area, we work in groups of 6. The 4 players inside start in the positions shown and we have 2 extra players outside. Each player moves to the next position after their actions.

Player 1 starts the exercise by passing out wide to player 2 who moves off the cone and passes inside to Player 3. Player 3 passes to 4 who moves off the cone and returns the ball straight back (one-two). Player 3 moves across and plays the ball into Player 4's path who moves across to receive the pass and play the ball back to the beginning. The practice continues.

Coaching Points

1. Create space before moving to meet the ball.

2. The correct open body shape should be monitored.

3. Change the direction of the sequence so that the players pass and receive with both feet.

Build Up Play, Quick Attacking Runs, Combination Play and Finishing

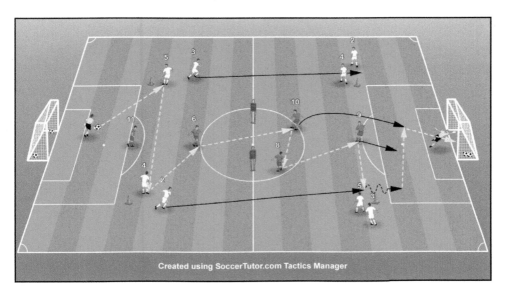

Created using SoccerTutor.com Tactics Manager

Objective

We work on tactical positioning and combination play on a full pitch.

Description

Using a full sized pitch we have the defenders in white, and the defensive midfielder (6), the 2 attacking midfielders (8 and 10) and striker (9) are in red.

The first white player (No.5 - centre back) passes the ball across the front of the penalty area to his teammate. When the second white centre back (4) receives he passes to the defensive midfielder (6). The 2 full backs (2 and 3) make forward runs.

The defensive midfielder combines with the attacking midfielders who pass to the striker (9). He passes to one of the full backs who have made runs forward. The full back who receives crosses the ball into the penalty area. The striker and the other full back run into the box to try to score.

The practice then starts again from the opposite end with 4 new white defenders.

Progression

Progress by adding 2 defenders against the 3 centre midfielders (reds) to create a 3v2 and also add a defender against the striker to create a 3v1 situation (including the 2 whites). This is an IPTE practice until you include aggressive opposition at which point it becomes an IPTETA drill. This drill can serve as a bridge between the warm up and main training session.

Dribbling Forwards to Draw in a Marker and Create Space for a Teammate

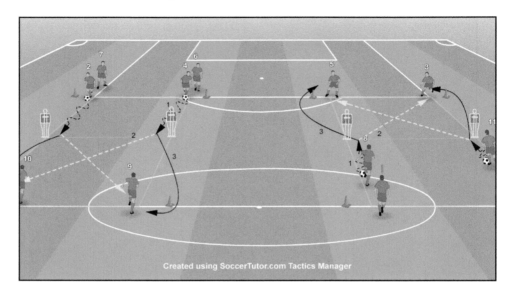

Objective

To practice dribbling the ball forwards to draw an opposition marker away from a teammate.

Description

In this practice we have two groups working simultaneously.

The first two players start at the same time with a ball each. They dribble the ball to the mannequin (or cone) directly in front of which represents an opponent. Just before they reach the 'defender' they play a diagonal pass to their teammate. The next two players then repeat the same sequence.

After the diagonal pass, the player moves to the position in front of him as shown in the diagram.

Coaching Point

This practice simulates a centre back dribbling the ball forwards to draw a marker away from his teammate, however all of the players take part as this action is important to our game model in other areas of the pitch as well.

Passing Across the Defensive and Midfield Lines

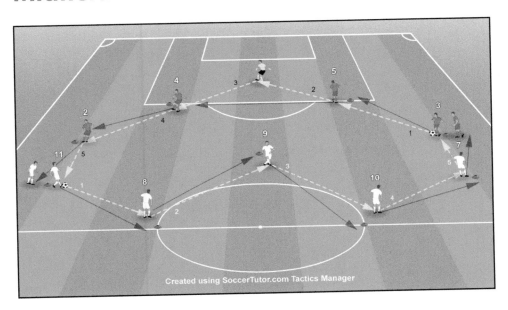

Created using SoccerTutor.com Tactics Manager

Objective

To develop the team's ability to pass along the midfield and defensive lines.

Description

The players are in their positions and we start with 2 balls simultaneously with the full back and the winger as shown in the diagram (No.3 and No.11). The 2 lines are facing each other.

The players all "pass and move", passing the ball through all of the positions and moving to the next position after each pass. In the defensive line there are 2 full backs, 2 centre backs and the goalkeeper. In the midfield line there are 2 wingers, 2 attacking midfielders and a striker (9).

The ball starts with one of the full backs and is passed along the line to the other full back who plays the ball to the winger in front of him. The winger moves forward and simulates that he is closed off so passes inside to the attacking midfielder (8) who passes to the striker (9). The ball is passed along the line to the other winger. He passes down the line to the full back and we start again.

Coaching Points

1. The players should play quickly with 1 or 2 touches.

2. Each player is able to learn the positioning, body shape and correct technique for passing and receiving in different positions across the line.

Quick Positional Combination Play to Switch the Play

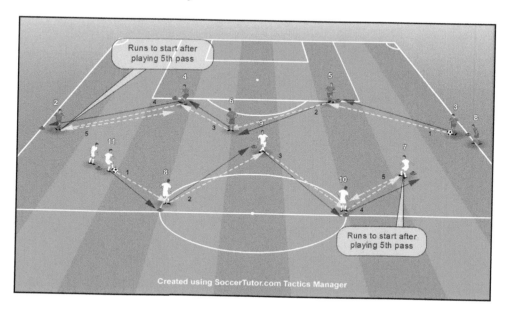

Objective

We work on player movement and switching play with quick passing combinations.

Description

Using half a full sized pitch, we have two lines of players facing each other again, but we have changed the position of the wingers slightly compared to the previous practice. This time the two lines work separately.

In the line closest to the penalty area we have 4 defenders and the defensive midfielder. In the attacking line we have 2 wingers, 2 attacking midfielders and the striker.

Start from the outside and the players move the ball inside then back across to start again. Each player moves to the next position after their pass, as shown in the diagram sequence. After the 5th pass, the wide player moves to the start position.

Positional Passing Square with Short and Long Support Play

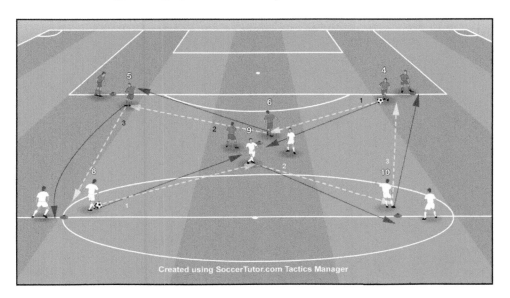

Created using SoccerTutor.com Tactics Manager

Objective

To improve short/long passing, combination play and timing of movement to provide support.

Description

In a 30 x 30 yard area we have 2 groups of 6 players working together in a passing combination exercise. The players start in their specific positions as shown. We start with 2 balls simultaneously in opposite corners, with the attacking midfielder and centre back respectively.

Attacking Sequence: The attacking midfielder (8) passes to the striker, who passes to the other attacking midfielder (10). The final pass is from the attacking midfielder (10) to the centre back (4) in the other group (this simulates a deep pass on the break to the winger or overlapping full back).

Defensive Sequence: The centre back (4) passes to the defensive midfielder (6) who passes to the other centre back (5). The sequence is completed with the final pass to the attacking midfielder (8) in the other group.

Coaching Points

1. For this passing sequence to be quick and flow efficiently, players should check away before moving to receive the pass which makes it easier for them to play with one touch.

2. The players and the ball should be constantly moving.

Quick Combination Play with Positional Inter-Changing of Diagonal Movements

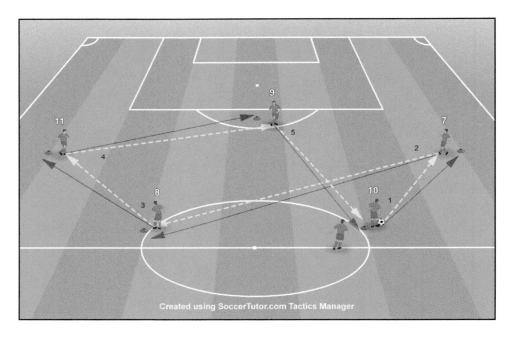

Created using SoccerTutor.com Tactics Manager

Objective

To practice attacking combination play and player movement in the opposition half.

Description

Using half a full sized pitch we work with 2 attacking midfielders, 2 wingers, 1 striker and an extra player. The players start in the positions shown in the diagram.

The ball starts with an attacking midfielder (10) who passes to the wide player (7) on that side. The winger, in turn, plays it to the other attacking midfielder (8) who then passes it to the winger closest to him on that side. The winger (11) passes to the striker (9) who passes back to the start where the extra player is waiting.

Each player moves to the next position after making a pass, as shown in the diagram.

Coaching Points

1. The players should check away from their cone to speed up play, trying to use one touch.

2. Each player should use the same body shape (protect the ball) and play quickly as if a direct opponent was closing them down.

Switching the Point of Attack with Player Movement in the Final Third

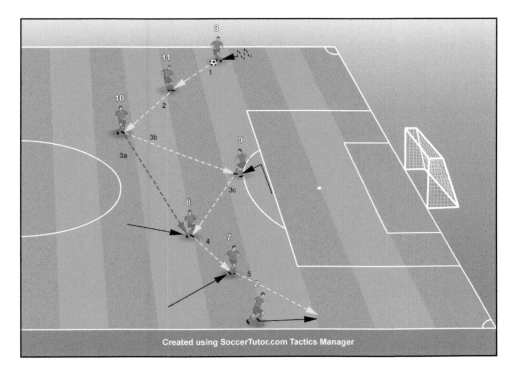

Created using SoccerTutor.com Tactics Manager

Objective

To develop player movement and combinations by switching the point of attack in the final third.

Description

We start on one side where the full back has been blocked off, simulating that the opposition have at least a numerical equality on the flank.

The full back (3) passes to the winger who passes to the attacking midfielder (10) who then links up with the other attacking midfielder (8). No.10 either passes directly to No.8 or the ball is moved via the striker No.9 (as shown in the diagram).

No.8 passes to the winger (7) who moves the ball out wide to the other full back (2). The full back crosses the ball as the players make runs into the box to try and score.

Repeat the practice starting from the opposite side with the right back (2).

Technical / Tactical Actions on the Wing: Dribble, Support Play & Finishing

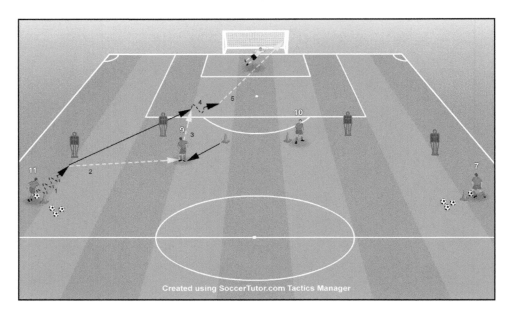

Objective

This practice is primarily for wingers to practice dribbling, quick combinations and finishing, with an emphasis on using their weaker foot.

Description

The winger dribbles towards the first coaching pole (which represents the opposing full back). The winger then moves inside and plays a one-two with the striker (or attacking midfielder) who moves off the cone to provide support.

The winger makes a run in behind the defence to receive the pass back, controls the ball inside the penalty area and tries to score.

Have this practice running on both sides of the pitch simultaneously.

Progression

Add defenders in place of the mannequins who apply passive resistance.

Technical / Tactical Actions for Attacking Through the Centre

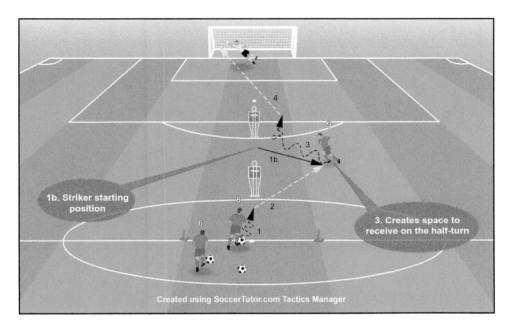

Objective

We use IPTE (interrelated physical-technical training methods) in this practice to work on the striker's movement, turning and finishing. .

Description

The centre midfielder (8) starts the practice by dribbling the ball forwards to the first mannequin or cone (representing an opponent) and passes to the striker who has performed a movement to "go dark" (moves to receive the ball in an area where his marker is unable to see both him and the ball simultaneously).

The striker receives on the half turn and dribbles past the other mannequin (also representing an opponent) and shoots at goal, trying to score past the goalkeeper..

Coaching Points

1. This practice is used to work on the striker dropping back to receive the ball in space, being aware to turn and then shoot at goal.

2. The striker must look over their shoulder before receiving the ball with their back foot and turning.

Physical, Technical and Tactical Practices (IPTETA)

Centre Backs: Building Up Play Through the Defensive Midfielder

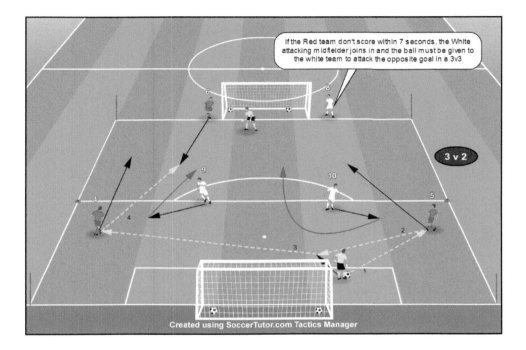

If the Red team don't score within 7 seconds, the White attacking midfielder joins in and the ball must be given to the white team to attack the opposite goal in a 3v3

3 v 2

Created using SoccerTutor.com Tactics Manager

Objective

We work with the centre backs who build up play from the back through the defensive midfielder under pressure from three opposition attackers (white).

Description

In an area double the size of the penalty box, we start with the read team's goalkeeper and he passes the ball to a centre back. The 2 white forwards apply pressure and try to win the ball. Once the 2 red centre backs and the goalkeeper have all touched the ball, the defensive midfielder can enter the game to create a 3v2 situation (plus the goalkeepers) and the aim is to score a goal as quickly as possible, exploiting the numerical advantage.

After 7 seconds of the red defensive midfielder (6) entering, the white attacking midfielder (8) enters the game to help the forwards and must be given the ball by the red team. The white team then attack the opposite goal with a 3v3 situation.

Coaching Point

Stress the importance to finish the attack within 7 seconds of the defensive midfielder entering, before the white attacking midfielder is allowed to enter (exploiting the numerical advantage).

Building Up from the Back with Interplay in Specific Zones on the Pitch

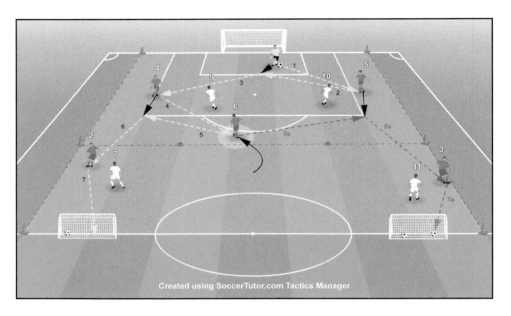

Created using SoccerTutor.com Tactics Manager

Objective

We work on the interplay and connection between the defence and the defensive midfielder, and the connection between the full back and winger - circulating the ball through these two zones.

Description

In a 40 x 55 yard area, the red defence starts with possession against the white attackers. The red defensive team consists of 6 players (goalkeeper, 2 centre backs, 2 full backs and 1 defensive midielder. The white attacking team consists of 4 players (1 striker, 1 attacking midfielder and 2 wingers.

Two players from each team are positioned in each zone, as shown in the diagram. The only player that can move across both zones is the red defensive midfielder (6).

For the ball to be played into zone 2, both centre backs (supported by the defensive midfielder) must have touched the ball. When the full back receives he must try and pass the ball into the small goal - simulating a pass out to the winger.

If the white attackers win the ball, they attack the big goal at the other end, trying to score past the goalkeeper.

Passing Out from the Back Within Position Specific Zones (6 v 6)

Objective

To practice passing out from the back within fixed positional roles.

Description

In this practice we play 6v6 in the area shown. We mark out five 2 x 2 yard squares. We have 4 red defenders and the defensive midfielder (6) who play against 5 white attackers (4-1 formation) who press to win the ball.

The red team aim to build up play and then score in the large goal past the goalkeeper. Before being allowed to shoot, the red defensive midfielder must touch the ball at least once. The defenders must receive the ball within their specific square. Once they have received the ball, they can then move out and play.

The attacking team (white) are not allowed to enter the squares, but can attempt to win the ball as soon as the defender or defensive midfielder leaves the square.

Coaching Points

1. The players must use an open body shape, receive with the back foot and have their heads up to see the next pass.

2. When combining with the defensive midfielder, the timing of the forward runs are key.

Dribbling Forwards to Create a Numerical Advantage in a Zonal Game

Created using SoccerTutor.com Tactics Manager

Objective

To work on dribbling the ball forwards to create a numerical superiority higher up the pitch. This practice is particularly useful to train the full backs, the centre backs and wingers to dribble forwards to create an attacking numerical superiority which the team can then exploit.

Description

We have two teams (7v7) in the same sized area as the previous practice. We mark out 3 equal zones as shown in the diagram with 2 players from each team in each zone.

The ball must be played from one zone to another with a player dribbling forwards. A player can only leave his zone by dribbling the ball across the line, thus creating a 3v2 situation in the next zone.

The team in possession aim to move the ball from zone 1 to zone 3 where they use their 3v2 numerical advantage to try and score a goal.

Coaching Points

1. The centre backs may need to create space (check away from their marker) before receiving.

2. An open body shape is required before receiving to be aware of the opponents.

3. The players need to be positive when dribbling away forwards into space.

Passing Along the Defensive/Midfield Lines in a Dynamic Transition Practice

Phase 1

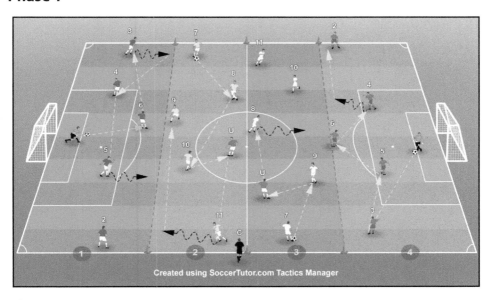

Phase 2

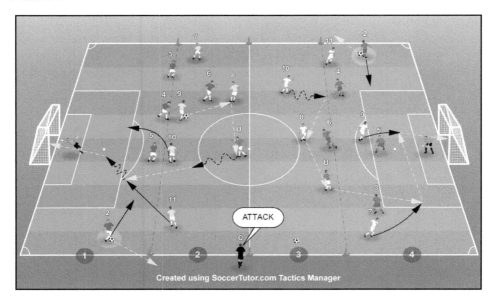

Objective

To develop technical aspects such as passing, body positioning and also practice transition play and attack vs defence.

Description

Using a full sized pitch, we mark out 4 equal zones as shown in the diagram. There is a line of 5 players in each zone.

In zones 1 and 4 we have 4 defenders and the defensive midfielder (red and blue players). In zones 2 and 3 we have the 4 other midfielders and the striker (yellow and white players).

Each line has a ball and the attacking lines have an extra neutral player (pink) to give them a numerical superiority.

Phase 1

Each line passes the ball, working specifically on technique - body positioning, quality of passes etc.

Phase 2

The defenders, who were passing the ball between themselves, kick their ball into touch and close up to prepare to defend an attack.

The teams in the middle (zones 2 and 3) attack the defenders and try to score a goal past the goalkeeper, with the help of the neutral player. This creates a 6 v 5 (+GK) attack vs defence situation.

The white team attack the reds and the yellow team attack the blues.

Coaching Points

1. It is important to progress with the ball and play "Expansive Football" to move the opponents and find gaps in their defence.

2. You can switch from phase 1 to phase 2 by blowing a whistle. This way the players have to react very quickly and take up their correct positional roles to either defend or attack.

"Expansive Football" Combination Play in a 7 v 2 Attack vs Defence Practice

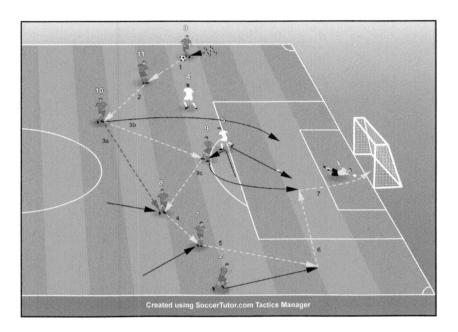

Created using SoccerTutor.com Tactics Manager

Objective

We practice attacking combinations and learn the movements needed to play "Expansive Football" with 2 active defenders to make it more problematic and game realistic.

Description

Using half a full sized pitch, we play 7v2. The red attackers have 2 attacking midfielders, 2 wingers, 2 full backs and the striker. The 2 white centre backs work together to defend the goal.

Start on one side, pretending that the full back (3) is blocked off. He passes to the winger (11) who passes to the attacking midfielder (10). The attacking midfielder can either pass to the other attacking midfielder (8) directly or via the striker (9).

When the second attacking midfielder (8) receives the ball he passes to the winger (7) on that side who plays it to the full back. The full back crosses the ball for one of the other players as they make runs into the box and escape the 2 defenders. Run the practice from both sides.

Coaching Points

1. The key to this is teaching the players the correct movements to play "Expansive Football".

2. The timing of the runs into the box and making sure to make intelligent movements away from the defenders will lead to more goals being scored.

"Expansive Football": Utilising the Full Backs in an Attack vs Defence 8 v 6 SSG

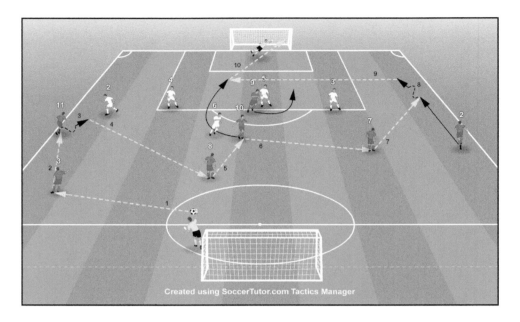

Created using SoccerTutor.com Tactics Manager

Objective

This is a simple but effective way of working on "Expansive Football" with the involvement of the full backs.

Description

We play a normal 8v6 small sided game. The red team start with the ball and have a numerical advantage to exploit and try to score. They have 2 full backs, 2 attacking midfielders, 2 wingers and a striker. The white defending team have 4 defenders and a defensive midfielder.

The attacking team try to use their numerical advantage to try and score. The whites defend their goal and try to win the ball. If they do, they counter attack and try to score at the other end.

Coaching Points

1. The emphasis is to use the full backs to exploit the numerical advantage.

2. The full backs can use overlapping or inside runs to create space or receive in behind the defence.

3. The numerical advantage can also be exploited by many players timing their runs into the penalty area for a cross.

Maintaining Possession in the Centre with Quick Break Attack and Finishing

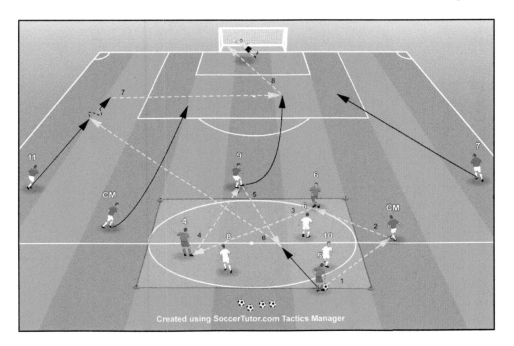

Created using SoccerTutor.com Tactics Manager

Objective

To practice maintaining possession in the centre of the pitch in a small space followed by a diagonal forward pass, crossing and finishing.

Description

Using a full pitch, we mark out a square in the middle as shown in the diagram. We have two teams of 3 players within the square. Outside the square we have 5 neutral players (2 centre midfielders, 2 wingers and 1 striker).

The 2 centre midfielders can and should play as support players for the players inside the square to maintain possession but they must not enter the square and are limited to 1 touch only.

When a team has played 4 passes inside the square (with support from the blue neutral players) they send a long, low ball out to the winger (to the left and No.11 in the diagram example).

All of the neutral players (centre midfielders, the striker and the opposite winger) make runs forward to meet the cross and try to score past the goalkeeper.

"Expansive Football" 10 v 10 Eight Goal Game

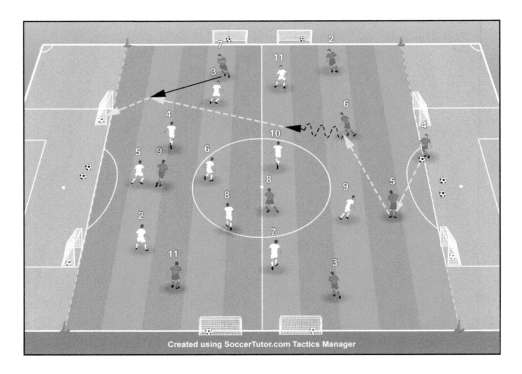

Created using SoccerTutor.com Tactics Manager

Objective

To work on the qualities of Expansive Football by maximising the width and depth of area.

Description

In the area between the two penalty boxes, we play a 10v10 game. Each team attacks 4 goals and defends the other 4. Both teams have the same aim, which is to build up play, create space and break down the other team's defence to score.

A goal scored in the wide goals are worth 1 point and goals scored in the goals at the edge of the penalty areas are worth 2 points.

Coaching Points

1. If the play is congested towards one side, encourage the team in possession to switch the play to the other side.

2. The need for the defenders to be aware of their positioning is increased as the team needs to defend all 4 goals.

Switching Play and "Expansive Football" in a 7 v 7 Game with Side Zones

Created using SoccerTutor.com Tactics Manager

Objective

To teach the importance of moving the ball from one side to the other to play "Expansive Football".

Description

Using half a full sized pitch, we mark out a central area the same width as the penalty box. We then have 2 side zones which the attacking team's full backs (2 and 3) occupy.

We play a normal small sided game with both teams trying to score but the team in possession have one full back positioned in each zone. No member of the defending team is allowed to enter either side zone. They can enter the penalty area once an attacker has moved in there.

The team in possession must pass the ball through each of the 3 zones (central zone, side zone and penalty area) before they are able to score. If the defending team win the ball, they must then also pass the ball through all 3 zones before scoring.

Coaching Points

1. As the team in possession has a numerical disadvantage in the central zone, they must look to move the ball quickly to the side zones.

2. The timing of the run for the cross is the key to scoring goals in this practice.

Creating a Numerical Advantage on the Flank with Side Zones in a 9 v 8 SSG

Objective

To work on an attack which switches the play to create 2v1 or 3v2 situations on the flanks.

Description

Using half a full sized pitch, we mark out 5 zones as shown. The red attacking team have 9 players (goalkeeper, 2 full backs, 1 defensive midfielder, 2 attacking midfielders, 2 wingers and 1 striker against a defensive team of 8 players (goalkeeper, 4 defenders, 1 defensive midfielder and 2 attacking midfielders.

The attacking team must pass the ball through all 3 channels and create a 2v1 or 3v2 situation out wide before scoring.

When the ball is in a wide zone the attacking team should have a minimum of 2 players (full back and winger) and a maximum of 3 in there (a midfielder joining). When they have a 2v1 or 3v2 and manage to enter the square near the byline (that no defenders can enter) they should play a high or low cross for the attackers to score.

If the ball is in one side zone, in the opposite side zone the attacking team should have a minimum of 1 player (winger) and a maximum of 2 with the full back in there.

If the attacking team have 2 players in a side zone, the defending team are only allowed 1 player. If the attacking team have 3 players in a side zone, the defending team are allowed to

have 2 players. The defending team are not allowed to have any players in the opposite side zone.

When the ball is in the central zone, the defending team are all grouped together there, leaving the full backs free in space out wide. No defender can enter the penalty area until an attacking player enters.

If the defending team win the ball they should perform a positional attack, making sure to pass the ball through the 3 channels before scoring. At this point there will be no restrictions in relation to the zones except for this.

Coaching Points

1. The player receiving within the wide zone should dribble inside to create space for the overlapping teammate.

2. The full back and winger on the opposite side to the play must not be in line with each other..

Utilising the Full Backs in Wide Positions in an 8 v 8 (+1) Small Sided Game

Created using SoccerTutor.com Tactics Manager

Objective

We work on the interplay and connection between defence, midfield and attack using the full backs to provide width in attack.

Description

In a 30 x 70 yard area, we mark out 3 zones as shown and play an 8v8 (+1 neutral player) game. The 2 end zones are 30 x 20 yards and the middle zone is 30 x 30 yards. In zone 1 there is the goalkeeper, 2 red centre backs and 2 white strikers. The defenders should try to dribble the ball out of zone 1 with a neutral player (who plays with the team in possession) in support.

When a defender reaches zone 2 he should pass to the full back outside him. When the full back receives, one opposing player can move outside to try and tackle him. The midfielder on the full back's team moves closer (staying within his zone) to receive a pass or play a one-two.

Both outside full backs must touch the ball before a goal can be scored. Only 2 defensive players (e.g. 2 centre backs) and 2 attackers (e.g. a midfielder and a striker) can enter zone 3. If the white team wins the ball, the two teams swap roles and vice versa if they lose it.

150

Switching Play Across the Back Line with Quick Transition Attacking Play

The Neutral Player Passes to the Reds (Transition)

COUNTER ATTACK

Created using SoccerTutor.com Tactics Manager

Objective

We work on the interplay and connection between the full backs and wingers, playing "Expansive Football" and transition play.

Description

Using an area slightly larger than half a full sized pitch, the white team have 8 players, the red team have 7 players and there are 2 neutral players (pink).

The white defence start with possession and the red attackers move across the pitch according to the position of the ball. The defenders circulate the ball against passive pressing from the reds.

When a full back connects with the neutral player (which would be the winger), the neutral player passes to a red attacking player and we have a transition. In the diagram example the neutral winger (7) passes to the red attacking midfielder (8).

As shown in the second diagram, the reds then start their attack and the neutral players move out wide to support them, trying to score a goal with an 8v7 situation outfield.

If the white team recover the ball they play with the neutral players to try and score in the goal at the opposite end.

The Midfielders and Striker Combining in a 3 v 2 Attacking Functional Practice

Objective

We work on the interplay between the 2 attacking midfielders and the striker in attack.

Description

In a 20 x 40 yard area, we play 3v2 with the 2 attacking midfielders and a striker against 2 defenders.

One attacking midfielder starts by passing to the striker who plays the ball back to the other attacking midfielder and together they attack the 2 defenders. The aim is to try and score quickly by exploiting the 3v2 numerical advantage.

When the attack is finished the 2 attacking midfielders stay where they are and become the defenders for the next group to attack. The 2 players who were defending become midfielders and take the ball and prepare to connect with the opposite number 9.

The Midfielders and Striker Combining in a 3 v 3 Attacking Functional Practice

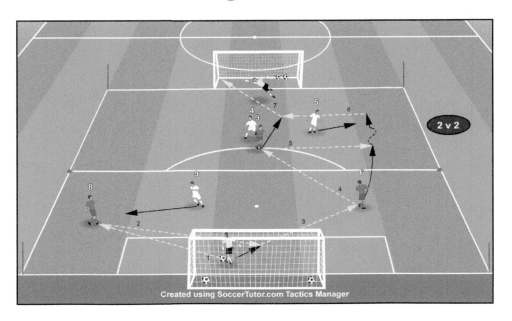

Created using SoccerTutor.com Tactics Manager

Objective

We work on the interplay between the 2 attacking midfielders and the striker in attack.

Description

In an area double the size of the penalty box, we play 4v4. The area is split into two equal zones. In the first zone the red team have 1 goalkeeper (who simulates being the defensive midfielder when in possession) and 2 attacking midfielders. The white team have a defensive midfielder who defends. The aim is to pass the ball forward to the red striker.

When the striker receives the ball, the attacking midfielder who passed the ball to him moves up to create a 2v2 situation in the second zone. The aim is to then combine and try to score past the goalkeeper. The 2 white centre backs defend the goal.

If a goal is scored, the goalkeeper makes a save or the ball goes out of play, then the team roles and positions are reversed with the white team attacking in the opposite direction.

Coaching Points

1. Both attacking midfielders and the goalkeeper must have touched the ball before the pass can be played to the striker.

2. The speed of play should be high and the full width of the area should be exploited.

Attacking Through the Centre in a 3 Zone Small Sided Game

Objective

We work on the interplay between the midfielders and the striker in a small sided game.

Description

This is a progression of the previous practice. In a 30 x 60 yard area we play a 7v7 game. The area is divided into three equal zones. Each team has a goalkeeper, 2 centre backs, 1 defensive midfielder, 2 attacking midfielders and 1 striker.

The 2 centre backs (4 and 5), the defensive midfielders (6) and the strikers (9) for each team must stay within the zone in which they are positioned. The attacking midfielders (8 and 10) are the only players who are allowed to move out of their respective zone.

The goalkeeper starts with the ball and the aim is to build up the play through the 3 zones and then score. When a midfielder successfully passes the ball to the striker then he or another midfielder can enter into the striker's zone to play a 2v2 and try to score.

Support Play for the Striker in a Zonal 7 v 7 (+3) Small Sided Game

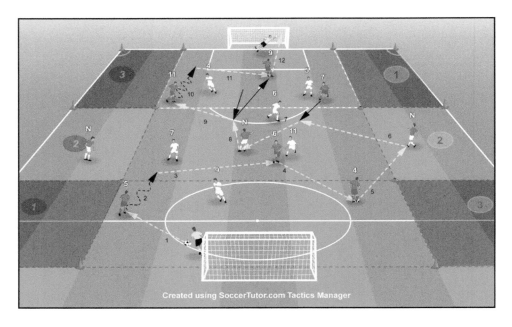

Created using SoccerTutor.com Tactics Manager

Objective

In this practice we work on movement to support the striker, allowing him to "go dark" (receive the ball in an area where his marker is unable to see both him and the ball simultaneously).

Description

In just the 3 central areas shown in the diagram, we play a 7v7 (+3 pink neutral players) small sided game. The 3 zones are divided as shown in the diagram and we also have 2 additional zones in use in which only the 2 wide neutral players are allowed. Both teams play using a 2-1-3 formation (2 defenders, 1 defensive midfielder and 3 forwards).

One goalkeeper starts the practice and the team in possession have 2 defenders in zone 1, the defensive midfielder in zone 2 and the 3 forwards in zone 3. They can only leave their zone in the following ways (the defending team can move freely):

1. A red defender can enter zone 2 by dribbling the ball forwards.
2. Once a defender has entered zone 2, the striker should also enter zone 2 in support.

Before a goal can be scored, 1 neutral player and the striker (within zone 2) must touch the ball. If the defending team win the ball, they should then play the ball quickly to their striker with help from the neutral player in zone 2 and create a 3v2 situation in the end zone to try and score (2 players move into the end zone to support the striker).

Possession Games for "Expansive Football" (IPTETA)

IPTETA METHOD POSSESSION DRILLS FOR EXPANSIVE FOOTBALL

In this section, we will demonstrate some "Expansive Football" IPTETA (interrelated physical-technical-tactical methods) directed at keeping possession of the ball.

Remember that the aim of "Expansive Football" is to keep possession in order to score a goal, but we can prioritise certain sub-objectives, in this case keeping possession. We have called these IPTETA drills "Mixture of Phases" as they incorporate all four phases of the game.

This IPTETA has been developed to be used on a Monday or Tuesday of the training week, for a period of active recuperation.

MIXTURE OF PHASES HEXAGON PRACTICE

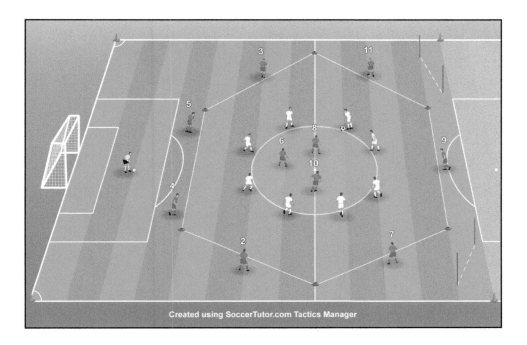

Created using SoccerTutor.com Tactics Manager

Description

The diagram above shows the template we are going to use for the 2 practices on the following pages.

Position the players like this:

- 1 goalkeeper with a big goal at one end and poles in the positions shown at the other end.

- 4 red defenders (2, 3, 4 and 5) in their specific positions they played in on match day.

- The 2 red attacking midfielders (8 and 10) and 1 defensive midfielder (6) that played in the match inside the centre circle.

- The 2 wingers (7 and 11) and striker (9) in the positions they play in on match day.

- 8 white players standing on the edge of the centre circle (those that played less than 65 minutes on match day.

The practices to follow will incorporate all four phases of the game. They will focus on possession play, pressing/tackling and the transition phases.

Dynamic 8 v 3 / 10 v 8 Possession Game with Transition Play

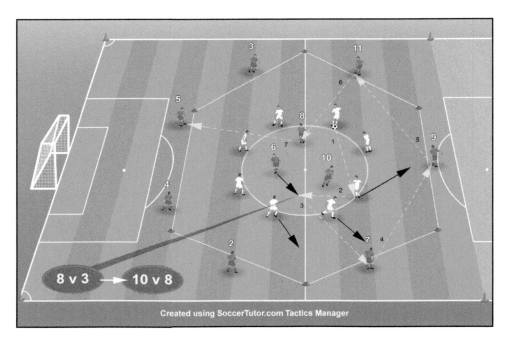

Created using SoccerTutor.com Tactics Manager

Description

Positioned around the centre circle we have 8 white players who aim to maintain possession but must not enter inside. The 3 red players inside (2 attacking midfielders and 1 defensive midfielder) work together to try and win the ball. This creates an 8v3 situation.

If the reds win the ball they pass to one of their teammates positioned along the outside of the hexagon. The game now moves into a larger area (the whole hexagon) with the reds in possession and the whites working together to try and win the ball back. The 3 reds in the middle can play within the area and the other 7 must stay on the outsides. This creates a 10v8 situation.

If the whites win the ball back from the reds, they then move back around the centre circle trying to maintain possession in an 8v3 situation.

Coaching Points

1. This practice works on the strength of the mobility of the whites.

2. If a bad pass is played but the opposition do not win the ball, make sure the players react quickly and try to maintain possession.

Counter Attacking in a Dynamic "Expansive Football" Possession Game

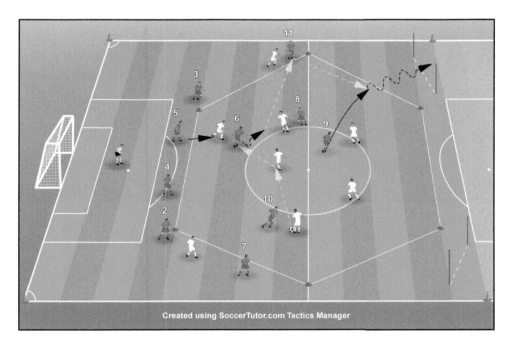

Created using SoccerTutor.com Tactics Manager

Objective

We work on maintaining possession, collective pressing/defending, tackling, counter attacking and quickly reacting as a team to transitions.

Description

This is a progression to the previous practice. The first two phases are exactly the same. We start with an 8v3 possession game in the centre circle. If the reds win the ball the practice changes to a 10v8 possession game.

The difference now is that if the whites win the ball back from the reds, they launch a counter attack towards the big goal and try to score.

The reds get into their tactical shape and defend the goal. If the reds can win the ball back again, they then attack (playing "Expansive Football") the opposite way and score by dribbling or shooting/passing through the poles at the sides of the pitch.

Positional Games

POSITIONAL GAME METHODS WITH PLAYER DIRECTIONALITY

The practices on the following pages are examples of positional games and are all directed at maintaining maximum possession of the ball, and using the game model and team's formation as a base.

The direction of the play dictates the players' positions.

Remember that there is no limit to the number of touches. The neutral players can be tackled and they should play within their areas marked out by the cones.

Positional 4 v 4 (+3) Possession Game: Passing Out Wide

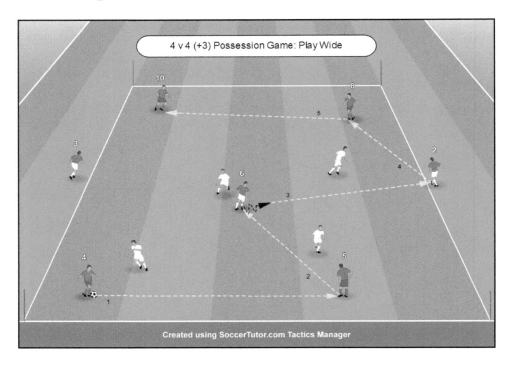

4 v 4 (+3) Possession Game: Play Wide

Created using SoccerTutor.com Tactics Manager

Objective

To practice maintaining possession within specific positional roles, focussing on width.

Description

In a 30 x 40 yard area, we play 4v4 (+3 neutral players). The neutral players out wide are the 2 full backs and the one in the middle is the defensive midfielder (6). The two teams (red and white) consist of the 2 centre backs and 2 attacking midfielders.

The team that has the ball must keep possession with the help of the neutral players. They should occupy their respective positions, both in attack and defence.

Coaching Points

1. The attacking team should open up the pitch and the defenders should close up the space.

2. This is a positional game in which we intersperse numerical superiority on the flanks with numerical superiority through the central channels; outside play with inside play. However, width is favoured.

Positional 4 v 4 (+3) Possession Game: Passing Through the Centre

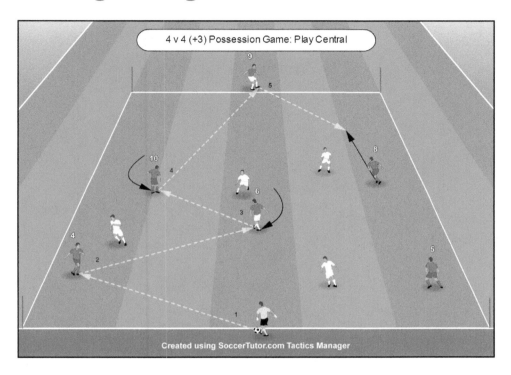

4 v 4 (+3) Possession Game: Play Central

Created using SoccerTutor.com Tactics Manager

Objective

In this variation to the previous practice we work on maintaining possession within specific positional roles, but this time the focus is on playing through the centre (from back to front).

Description

In a 30 x 40 yard area, we play 4v4 (+3 neutral players). The neutral players at each end are the goalkeeper (1) and the striker (9) and the defensive midfielder (6) is in the middle. The two teams (red and white) consist of the 2 centre backs and 2 attacking midfielders.

The team that has the ball must keep possession with the help of the neutral players. They should occupy their respective positions, both in attack and defence. The goalkeeper is not allowed to touch the ball with his hands.

Coaching Points

1. The attacking team should open up the pitch and the defenders should close up the space.

2. This is a positional game in which we create a numerical superiority through the central channels, making sure to utilise the defensive midfielder (6).

Positional 7 v 7 (+3) Possession Game: Passing Out Wide & Through the Centre

7 v 7 (+3) Possession Game: Play Wide and Central

Created using SoccerTutor.com Tactics Manager

Objective

To practice maintaining possession, trying to create a numerical superiority in the centre or out wide and interspersing outside and inside play within positional roles.

Description

In a 40 x 60 yard area, we play 7v7 (+3 neutral players). The neutral players are the 2 wingers (11 and 7) and the defensive midfielder (6) in the middle. The two teams (red and white) consist of 2 centre backs, 2 full backs, 2 attacking midfielders and 1 striker.

The team that has the ball must keep possession with the help of the neutral players.

Coaching Points

1. The players should occupy their respective positions, both in attack and defence.

2. It is important to fully utilise the neutral players (through the centre and out wide) to exploit the 10v3 numerical advantage to maintain possession.

Positional 6 v 6 (+4) Possession Game: Building Up Play from Back to Front

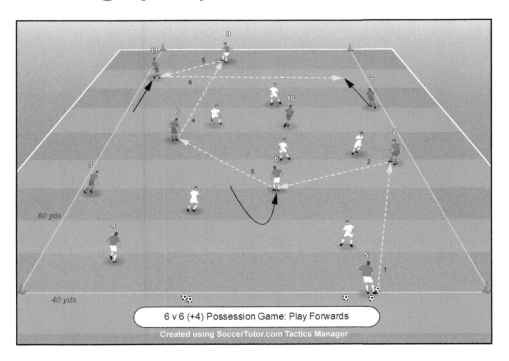

60 yds

40 yds

6 v 6 (+4) Possession Game: Play Forwards

Created using SoccerTutor.com Tactics Manager

Objective

This positional game gives us continuous depth (playing forwards) in both the defensive and attacking phases.

Description

In a 40 x 60 yard area, we play 6v6 (+4 neutral players). The neutral players are the 2 centre backs (4 and 5), the defensive midfielder (6) and the striker (9). The two teams (red and white) consist of the 2 full backs, the 2 attacking midfielders and the 2 wingers.

The team that has the ball must keep possession with the help of the neutral players. They should occupy their respective positions, both in attack and defence.

Positional Games with Finishing

POSITIONAL GAMES WITH FINISHING

The following examples of positional games are all directed at scoring in one or more goals. The goals can be interchanged each time one is scored. We will also look at how to conquer space.

Personally, we like to relate the two, meaning that we start in one space and play the ball until we arrive in another space where there is a goal.

Scoring a goal is the ultimate objective of all attacking moves.

Combining with the Striker & Finishing in a Dynamic 4 v 4 (+3) Positional Game

Objective

This is a positional game that focuses on playing the ball forwards through the centre and the connection with the striker in order to score a goal.

Description

In a 30 x 80 yard area, we play 4v4 (+3 neutral players). The two teams (red and white) consist of the 2 centre backs and 2 centre midfielders and they are positioned in the 30 x 40 yard central zone. The neutral players at each end are the goalkeeper (1) and the striker (9) and the defensive midfielder (6) is in the middle.

When the team in possession have played a minimum of five passes (with the neutral player's participation) they can then pass the ball to the neutral striker (9) who turns and enters the end zone, trying to score past the goalkeeper.

Every time a goal is scored, the ball goes out of play or a team wins the ball, the roles of the teams are reversed and the practice continues.

Attacking Through the Centre in a 6 v 6 (+4) Positional Game

Created using SoccerTutor.com Tactics Manager

Objective

This is a positional game that focuses on playing the ball always towards the goal and the connection with the striker in order to score.

Description

In a 50 x 70 yard area, we play 6v6 (+4 neutral players). This is a positional game where the team in possession should always play towards the goal and try to score. The players must stay within their zones. In zone 1 we have a 3v1 situation, in the middle we have a 3v3 situation and in the final zone we have a 3v1 situation again.

There is a 3v3 situation in the centre of the pitch (3 midfielders from each team) who aim to connect with the striker (9) in the end zone. When they connect with him the striker they can look to score with the support of two neutral players creating a 3v1 situation

If the defending team win the ball, they then attack in the opposite direction with help from the neutral players with the same rules applied.

Connecting the Defence, Midfield and Attack in a Positional 9 v 9 Zonal Game

Objective

This is a positional game that focuses on the inter-zonal connection between defence, midfield and attack and the finishing of the three attackers.

Description

In a 55 x 75 yard area, we play a 9v9 game. This is a positional game where the team in possession should always play towards the goal and try to score.

Both teams have a goalkeeper, 2 centre backs (4 and 5), 2 attacking midfielders (8 and 10), 1 defensive midfielder (6), 2 wingers (7 and 11) and 1 striker (9) using a 2-3-3 formation.

We mark out a central zone with cones as shown where there is a 3v3 situation. The first aim is for one of the centre backs to dribble the ball into the central zone giving them a 4v3 advantage to combine and attack through the centre.

In the attacking zone for the team in possession there is a 3v2 advantage. The aim is to pass the ball to a winger or the striker and using their 3v2 advantage they try to score in the goal past the goalkeeper.

CHAPTER 10

CONCLUSION

CONCLUSION

We have come to the conclusion of our book, but football never ends. We must always be open to change and evolution and how welcome it will be! These changes mean the arrival of new players and innovative coaches who are always recycling, forming and searching for new football strategies.

The situations that we have created must always have these three fundamental characteristics, that they are combative, cooperative and cognitive. *"If our players legs are tired from running then their brains must also be tired from thinking".* It is very important to realise that a player learns not only through what he is told, but through what he does. This is why it is vital that we select and work on the right situations and drills/practices.

"Expansive Football" is a style of football which must be based on the characteristics, interactions and nature of our players. We saw the importance of Oscar Cano's principle of complementarity; to have players who play similarly, understand the tactical team play, have great interaction, synergy and assertive-drive between them and are not just technically excellent.

To work on this type of football, these specific drills and methods must be adapted to suit the player and the team and vice versa without culling their creativity. This is why we have never limited the number of touches etc. The footballer will improve little by little and will help his teammates improve through the idea of sub-optimal behaviours (Rafel Pol quoted by R. Moreno). This idea is based on the fact that the players try harder to put themselves at the same level as those around them. Imagine if you were Xavi and I am Iniesta and next to us we have Messi. If the drills are effective we will improve and compete to show our worth (through work on

the emotional-will sphere, trying to improve and achieve the drill's objective). This is why these three superstars from Barcelona are repeatedly winning awards and in 2011 won the Balon D'Or and the silver and bronze prizes between them.

This is why both the players and the coaches always have to aim for excellence. This is achieved through hard work, as Jorge D'Alessandro says, *"a minimum of two hours a day at the desk",* thinking of new drills, watching videos etc. You only achieve excellence by giving 100% to the work and by being as self-demanding as possible.

This sport is great not just for the game itself, but for everything that is found within it on the pitch. A team's socio-affectivity impregnates them, you can see and feel it. Football is a "micro-struggle" within a "macro-confrontation", but through the interactions and socio-affectivity we should never feel alone, not in attack or defence. We will always be looked after by a teammate at any given moment within any phase.

"Expansive Football" can seem like a type of lineal attacking football, but because of the unpredictability of the players, this is exactly what it is not. It is the players, with their qualities that make it unpredictable.

Football belongs to the footballers. Us coaches should simply let them be and guide them towards what they can become and achieve. You already know that the work of a coach is hard and sometimes a thankless task. The results shape the destiny of the manager but winning is a consequence of the coach's good work.

As coaches we must feel the same way as Christopher Columbus. He firmly believed in a new world and had an incredibly strong vision but nobody believed him until one

day when, through the intervention of Queen Isabel, those three boats set sail - La Niña, la Pinta and la Santa Maria. We should not be scared of innovation. To discover "new worlds" we must have courage and the strength to believe in what we are doing, to never lose this. We should remain faithful to our vision, to what we feel, and despite waves or storms that could defeat us we must never lose hope. We should remain motivated throughout our journey with high morale running through our team.

Many of the theories that we invent could seem absurd, but everything starts with something absurd. Who believed in Sacchi's offside principle? Or Guardiola's "false nine"? It will be, as F. Guccini says, *"An absurd battle at best, but we cannot ignore it. It is the absurd that makes us proud to be ourselves".* If we have a vision and we absolutely believe in it and follow the idea blindly it will eventually become reality. If we can get the best out of ourselves, feel satisfied in spite of the results, then we can really feel proud of ourselves. The results should not steal our dreams - if you take a man's dreams away then what does he have left?

"Expansive Football" is a recipe for a positional attack within a game model, a way to play the good, attacking football that grows within our footballers. We warn you that it does not guarantee that you will win but you will be closer to victory with an attractive and lively game. That is one of the aims of football, to let the spectators enjoy the game and identify with the type of game their team is playing. It is not only for the fans of your team but others as well because we are all in love with this incredible game.

Whatever happens, we cannot stop believing in our ideas, in ourselves, our players and most of all, in the journey.

"And go as if pushed by destiny towards a war,

Towards adventure, and return against all prophecy, against the gods and against fear"

"In the 99th year of our life,
I, troubadour by nothing, but indignant,

Here I sing in a weary voice,

With an exhausted roar,

But I dedicate these nothing words,

To an old underlying habit,

Hoping, but, that you do not find them ridiculous,

Thou, hypocritical reader, my fellow,

My friend..."

(F. Guccinin, Addio).

THANK YOU

I would like to thank Paco Cordobés for giving me the opportunity to write this book and for inviting me to express the ideas I carry in my head and for compiling those that I took to my training sessions.

Thanks for the football conversations with my learned friends in this fantastic game and in life:

- Paco Cordobés (Director ABFutbol)
- Pedro Gómez (author of the book La Preparación física del fútbol contextualizada en el fútbol)
- Rubén Sánchez López de Toro (coordinator of grassroots football at CF Liceo Sport)
- Agustín Lleida (physical trainer at Pachuca de México)

I also want to mention Alfredo Sebastiani (on the coaching staff at Watford) for his kindness and courtesy in sharing his ideas and opinions, not only about "Expansive Football" but about football in general, and Manuel Conde for making me believe that human creativity knows no bounds.

And thanks obviously to Eloi Martinez, the man who taught me the art of coaching and the magic of football.

I also want to give thanks to all of those people in both football and in life that I have not mentioned but have influenced me, who have helped me to grow as a coach and as a person. To all of those teams that I have coached, and to the last two teams I have been with: Cadet B of EFValls and the Alevín team at D Gimnastic de Tarragona - both of which have shown me much about football and life, making me feel like a coach to the elite.

And obviously, thank you to my Mercè, the girl that I love who always supports me through difficult times, her respect and most of all, her patience towards my second love, football.

Lastly, thank you very much for buying this book and I hope you found it very useful.

Pasquale Casà Basile

BIBLIOGRAPHY

BIBLIOGRAPHY

- Manuel Conde Transición Ataque-Defensa, Pautas Táctico-Emocionales. Ed. MCSports, 2010

- Manuel Conde, Fútbol Camino al Éxito tomo I, II, III, IV, V y VI. Ed. Supérate, 2009...

- Pedro Gómez, libro La Preparación física del fútbol contextualizada en el fútbol. Ed. MCSports, 2011

- Rafel Pol, libro La Preparación ¿física? en el fútbol. Ed. MCSports, 2011

- X. Tamarit, libro Periodización Táctica vs Periodización Táctica. Ed. MBF, 2013

- Sanz y Frattarola, libro Los Fundamento del Juego, Programa AT-3, Etapa de Rendimiento Ed. MCSports, 2009

- X. Tamarit, libro ¿Que es la Periodización Táctica? Ed. MCSports, 2007

- B. Oliveira, N. Amieiro, N. Resende, R. Barreto: libro Mourinho ¿Porqué tantas victorias? Ed. MCSports, 2007

- Xesco Espar, libro Jugar con el corazón. Ed. Plataforma editorial, 2010

- José Maria Buceta, libro Estrategias psicológicas para entrenadores de deportistas jóvenes, Ed. Dykinson, 2004

- M. Monteleone y M.A. Ortega Jiménez, libro La construzione di un Modello di gioco, Ed. Allenatore.net, 2013

- Robert Moreno, libro Mi receta del 4-4-2 Ed. FutboldeLibro 2013

- Maurizio Viscidi, libro I giochi di posizione, I Moderni possessi palla per ruolo, Ed. Allenatore.net, 2011

- Alberto Gonzalez, libro Fútbol, dinámica del juego desde la perspectiva de las tansiciones, ed. Learning11, 2013

- Varias Revistas, Videos de Cursos On-line y Suplementos de la Revista AB Fútbol

- Videos de Cursos On-line de la Escuela de formación de entrenadores Fútbol Lab

- Videos de Cursos On-line de la Escuela de formación de entrenadores Learning11

- Francesco Guccini, Ritratti, cd musical ed. EMI, 2004

- Francesco Guccini, Addio, cd musical ed. EMI, 2000

CPSIA information can be obtained at www.ICGtesting.com
Printed in the USA
BVOW11s0453141115

427087BV00009B/48/P